ARNOLD'S

ENGLISH

TEXTS

General Editor JAMES SUTHERLAND
Lord Northcliffe Professor of Modern English Literature
University College, London

EARLY EIGHTEENTH CENTURY POETRY

Edited by
JAMES SUTHERLAND

*Lord Northcliffe Professor of Modern English Literature,
University College, London*

EDWARD ARNOLD (PUBLISHERS) LTD.
41 Maddox Street, London W.1

C

245749

English

Printed in Great Britain by
The Camelot Press Ltd., London and Southampton

General Preface

THE design of this series is to present fully annotated selections from English literature which will, it is hoped, prove satisfactory both in their breadth and their depth. To achieve this some of the volumes have been planned so as to provide a varied selection from the poetry or prose of a limited period, which is at once long enough to have developed a literary movement and short enough to allow for adequate representation of the chief writers and of the various cross-currents within the movement. Examples of such periods are the late seventeenth century and the early eighteenth century. In other volumes the principle of selection is to present a literary kind (e.g. satirical poetry, the literary ballad). Here it is possible to cover a longer period without sacrificing the unified and comprehensive treatment which is the governing idea for the whole series. Other volumes, again, are designed to present a group of writers who form some kind of "school" (e.g. the Elizabethan sonneteers, the followers of Ben Jonson), or who were closely enough linked for their work to be brought together (e.g. the poetry of Johnson and Goldsmith).

Each volume has a full critical introduction. Headnotes, a special feature of this series, provide relevant background and critical comment for the individual poems and prose pieces. The footnotes are for the most part explanatory, giving as briefly as possible information about persons, places, allusions of one kind or another, the meaning of words, etc., which the twentieth-century reader is likely to require. Each selection aims at providing examples of the best work of the authors represented, but it is hoped that the inclusion of some less familiar pieces not available in any other collection will widen the reader's experience and enjoyment of the literature under review. The series is intended for use in universities and the upper forms of schools.

In this collection of early eighteenth-century poetry the editor has aimed at including as many of the different "kinds" as possible, so as to do justice to the range and variety of the poetry written during the period. Examples will accordingly be found of the mock-heroic, georgic, ode, elegy, epistle, verse tale, character, "night piece", hymn, song, ballad, epigram, prologue, as well as translations and imitations, and a poem such as James Thomson's *Winter* for which the eighteenth century had not yet found a generic term. The poets most fully represented are naturally those of most importance—Pope, Swift and Gay; but more than a dozen of the minor poets are also included. It is hoped that this selection will demonstrate not only the wit and high finish of the best eighteenth-century poetry, but also the way in which the poets contemplated the life of their own day, and how they ordered their experience of it. Unless otherwise stated, the text follows that of the first edition of each poem; but some changes in punctuation have been made, and italics for such words as "London", "Jove", etc., have been replaced by roman.

Contents

Introduction

FORTY or fifty years ago it would have been necessary to introduce such a volume as this with some sort of special pleading. The reputation of Pope and his contemporaries was then at a low ebb. In so far as Pope himself was still generally read it was probably in the "Globe" edition of 1869, whose editor, Sir A. W. Ward, tried to make out a brave case for Pope but was clearly embarrassed by imperfect sympathy with his author. There were twentieth-century editions of Prior, Swift and Gay; but the work of these poets evoked little critical comment, and it must be assumed that they were not much read. All four poets retained only a slender foothold in such representative collections as *The Oxford Book of English Verse* (1900): in a volume of nearly 1,100 pages Prior was given $5\frac{1}{2}$, Pope, $3\frac{1}{2}$, Gay, half a page, and Swift was not represented at all. In Palgrave's *Golden Treasury* (1861), which continued to circulate widely in the early years of the present century, the eighteenth-century poets fared even worse, and were represented mainly by Gray, Collins, Cowper and Burns. It is true that both Palgrave and Quiller-Couch were concentrating on lyrical poems, but in any case the kind of poetry then most in favour was not the kind usually cultivated by Pope and his contemporaries.

The taste of the reader of poetry in 1900 was not very different from that of Lamb or Coleridge a century earlier, except that it was perhaps rather less inclusive. The poets and critics of the early nineteenth century had done their work so well that, with certain modifications, their view of what was and what was not poetry was still dominant. Ever since Wordsworth had come to be recognised as a great poet, a new emphasis had fallen on external Nature as a subject for poetry; on trees and flowers and birds, mountains and lakes and cataracts—on the whole world of natural phenomena, both animate and inanimate, seen and felt by Wordsworth himself not as a mere background to human life, but as the immediate expression of the "wisdom and spirit of the universe". In his pantheistic attitude to Nature Wordsworth was quite exceptional, and few of his contemporaries came anywhere near to cultivating that "wise passiveness" which he advocated, or to sharing in his almost mystical sense of identity with the natural world. None the less, he had succeeded in giving nature poetry a remarkable prestige, and it became almost an article of poetic faith that to write about daffodils and nightingales and waterfalls was to write poetry. As late as the 1920's the

Georgian poets were still making their pleasant excursions into the country-side, and returning with what was largely a poetry of walking-tours and rural week-ends, of nicely observed and pleasantly recorded natural phenomena. To Stopford Brooke, an elderly but representative critic of the early twentieth century, it seemed self-evident that there were two great subjects of poetry, Nature and human nature; and he went on to add: "When Pope was writing, the love of Nature for itself had quite decayed."

That Nature was by no means so dead as all that in the early eighteenth century may be seen from some of the poems in this volume. Yet it is only right to add that the notion of Nature being one of the two great subjects of poetry would not have commended itself to many of Pope's contemporaries, either because they had not thought of it that way, or because they would have actively disagreed. When Thomson's *Winter* was published in 1726 its originality was soon realised, but at least one distinguished reader (no doubt representative of many more) found *The Seasons* unsatisfactory. In a letter written in 1732 Swift remarked that too many "vile hands" had been writing in blank verse of late, and he added: "One Thomson, a Scotchman, has succeeded the best in that way, in four poems he has wrote on the four seasons, yet I am not over fond of them, because they are all description, and nothing is doing, whereas Milton engages me in actions of the highest importance. . . ." Swift's complaint recalls Pope's estimate of his own early poetry, in which, he thought, "pure description held the place of sense". *The Seasons* was a long poem, and for the eighteenth-century reader a long poem ought to have an action, or should at least deal with human concerns. The proper study of mankind, and therefore of the poet, was man. This view of poetry was not peculiar to the eighteenth century; it had been the normal view since the time of Aristotle onwards. "Human affairs and human feelings," wrote James Beattie, a middle-of-the-road critic of the later eighteenth century,

> are universally interesting. . . . Mere descriptions, however beautiful . . . become tiresome, where our passions are not occasionally awakened by some event that concerns our fellow-men.

Beattie's objection is, of course, to "mere descriptions"; neither he nor any other eighteenth-century critic would have objected to incidental passages of description introduced as the setting for a poem, or by way of illustration or embellishment. When Thomson enlarged *The Seasons* some of his additions were designed to supply more human interest, and Wordsworth is an unwilling witness to their popularity. In any well-used copy of *The Seasons*, he remarked, "the book generally opens of itself with the rhapsody on love, or with one of the stories (perhaps 'Damon and Musidora')".

When descriptive passages appear in eighteenth-century poetry—and they are much more frequent than is sometimes supposed—modern readers are still apt to find something wanting because they are looking for what the poet as often as not deliberately avoided giving his readers. On the whole, he accepted the view of Johnson that the poet is not "to number the streaks of the tulip, or describe the different shades in the verdure of the forest". When Wordsworth asserted that Pope and his contemporaries appeared to have written without having their eye fixed steadily on their object he was saying what he could not possibly know, and he was assuming that if a description was in general terms and not minutely particularised the poet could not really have looked at what he was describing. But he could and did: the difference lies in the way that he dealt with the *data* of observation. Perhaps the clearest exposition of the eighteenth-century attitude to the general and the particular is to be found in the *Discourses* that Sir Joshua Reynolds gave to his students at the Royal Academy. For Reynolds, art deals with the general, the typical, the ideal:

> I remember a landscape-painter in Rome, who was known by the name of "Studio", from his patience in high finishing, in which he thought the whole excellence of art consisted; so that he once endeavoured, as he said, to represent every individual leaf on a tree. . . . A landscape-painter certainly ought to study anatomically (if I may use the expression) all the objects which he paints; but when he is to turn his studies to use, his skill, as a man of genius, will be displayed in showing the general effect, preserving the same degrees of hardness and softness which the objects have in nature; for he applies himself to the imagination, not to the curiosity, and works not for the Virtuoso or the Naturalist, but for the common observer of life and nature.

The painter, then, is to have a detailed knowledge of the objects that he paints; but he must know what is essential, and what—because it is *not* essential—he should leave out. No doubt the process of abstraction can be carried too far; but certainly the best eighteenth-century poets knew how to concentrate on the essential without losing that sharpness of impact which anything fully realised has on the consciousness. When Dyer, the author of *The Fleece*, writes of the

> prickly Bramble, white with woolly Theft,

he is giving us all that we need to know in order to visualise the blackberry bush with wisps of wool caught from passing sheep, and he is reinforcing the impression by the phrase "woolly theft", which at once stimulates our attention by its packed significance, and suggests the softness and lightness of wool by the sound of the words, contrasting with the hard vowels and consonants of "prickly bramble". So, too, Pope's lines in "Spring"—

> Soon as the Flocks shook off the nightly Dews,
> Two Swains, whom Love kept wakeful, and the Muse,
> Pour'd o'er the whitening Vale their fleecy Care . . .

set before our eyes the general appearance of a flock of sheep spreading out over a valley, but do this vividly by his individual application of the word "pour'd" to the flowing and continuous movement of the sheep, and (as one of his eighteenth-century commentators noted) by the progressive effect of the word "whitening".

By virtue of his generalised descriptions the eighteenth-century poet frequently achieved an effect that was then much sought after: that "greatness" (grandeur) which Johnson associated with "positions not limited by exceptions, and descriptions . . . not descending to minuteness". That was the theory: it was constantly borne out in practice, as in Pope's vision of an England despoiled by the Norman conquerors:

> The levell'd Towns with Weeds lie cover'd o'er,
> The hollow Winds thro' naked Temples roar;
> Round broken Columns clasping Ivy twin'd;
> O'er Heaps of Ruin stalk'd the stately Hind;
> The Fox obscene to gaping Tombs retires,
> And savage Howlings fill the sacred Quires. . . .

or, in a comparable passage, where he is writing about the dark ages:

> Lo where Mæotis sleeps, and hardly flows
> The freezing Tanais thro' a waste of Snows.

A similar grand effect is often obtained by the personified abstractions so frequent in the poetry of the period. Eighteenth-century theory and practice, then, tended to favour the abstract because it meant a concentration on the essential, and to favour the general because (as Reynolds argued) the whole beauty and grandeur of art depended upon getting above "all singular forms, local customs, particularities, and details of every kind". For the modern mind, accustomed to a literature that deals with the individual, the peculiar, the abnormal, even the unique, some adjustment is required in approaching neo-classical poetry. But the differences should not be exaggerated. Although the views of Reynolds are fairly representative of the whole period, he went a good deal further than most of his contemporaries in his condemnation of the individual and particular. In some forms of literature, e.g. prose fiction, the generalising habit is much less prominent; it is certainly present in Fielding, but is at a minimum in Richardson.

In poetry the practice varies with the kind. Much of the satirical poetry, for example, was directed against specific evils, excesses, abuses, follies, as in Pope's description of Timon's villa, and frequently against individual persons, as in his character of Addison. Yet even here, although we are made sharply aware of the individual, the general truth keeps shining through.

By ignoring "the minuter discriminations which one may have remarked and another neglected", and by avoiding or suppressing many of those thoughts and feelings and observations which might be too individual to be common property, the eighteenth-century poet was able to appeal confidently to the experience of the average man. Behind this appeal lay the widespread belief that literature deals (better, of course, than we can do for ourselves) with what oft was thought, felt, observed. Behind this again lay the belief that the pleasure to be derived from literature is largely one of delighted recognition, of being able to confirm from one's own experience the truth of what one has just read. "Wit and fine writing," Addison once observed, paraphrasing Boileau,

> doth not consist so much in advancing things that are new, as in giving things that are known an agreeable turn. It is impossible for us, who live in the latter ages of the world, to make observations in criticism, morality, or in any art or science, which have not been touched upon by others. We have little else left us, but to represent the common sense of mankind in more strong, more beautiful, or more uncommon lights.

Those words occur in a *Spectator* essay (No. 253) in which Addison gives some well-deserved praise to Pope's *Essay on Criticism*. The thoughts, he observes, are for the most part not new at all, but they "are placed in so beautiful a light, and illustrated with such apt allusions, that they have in them all the graces of novelty, and make the reader who was before acquainted with them still more convinced of their truth and solidity". One example will be enough to prove Addison's contention. As it leaves Pope's hands, the old thought that it is no use disputing about tastes comes over in a new and brilliant expression:

> 'Tis with our Judgments as our Watches, none
> Go just alike, yet each believes his own.

The *Essay on Criticism* abounds with passages such as this that give the charm of novelty to thoughts of every day. When the transformation is made as brilliantly as this, the "little else left us" that Addison talks about is surely a good deal.

One last distinction must be made between the neo-classical poets and those who came after them. The eighteenth-century poet thought of poetry as an art, and when he wrote he was not so much concerned with writing poetry as with making poems. The great Romantic poets were very far from being without art, but the whole tendency of the Romantic period was to lay stress on the natural, the unstudied, the spontaneous (never were there so many Voluntary Effusions and extempore Lines Written on a Beautiful Evening or Left upon a Seat), and to show a corresponding distrust of art. In due course the poetry of the eighteenth century was held to be artificial, which it often was; but the words "artificial" and "artificiality", instead of being purely descriptive, acquired a pejorative meaning. There was much talk of mechanical regularity and the monotony of the heroic couplet; worse still, the poets were accused of writing, not for mankind, but only for the fashionable and the polite, those whom Wordsworth described as "the wealthy Few", and whom he thought of as being characterised by artificial manners and an unfeeling remoteness from human concerns. So far as the form and structure of eighteenth-century poetry is concerned, the neo-classical balance and regularity were also to be found in the music, the architecture, the painting, the dance, and even the conversation of the period. We can surely respect a taste that gave us Wren's churches, Handel's music and *The Rape of the Lock* and the conversation of Dr. Johnson, even if modern taste is more likely to favour freedom and irregularity. The other charge, that eighteenth-century poetry was addressed mainly to the polite and sophisticated reader, cannot be answered by an indignant denial; but, on the other hand, it does not call, *pace* Wordsworth, for any moral defence. Lord Chesterfield and Horace Walpole were quite as worthy of consideration as Goody Blake or Simon Lee, and on many not unimportant matters were a good deal better informed.

Eighteenth-century poetry, then, is often artificial in the sense that the poet is primarily interested in composing a poem, which will almost certainly belong to one of the recognised "kinds", and which will therefore be controlled by that fact and will be written in a style conformable to the expectations of a cultured reader. The poet will be making use of human activities with the detachment of an artist who is standing well back from the object of his contemplation, and who is less concerned with expressing the raw material of life than with perfecting the stylised composition on which he is engaged. This is so with Pope in *The Rape of the Lock*, and it is especially so with the author of *Trivia*. Gay revelled in the delicate absurdities of poetic diction and the mock-heroic possibilities of classical allusion; and he adapted and modified the eighteenth-century scene to suit his own poetic idiom, just as the painter Henri Rousseau created his formalised tropical landscapes in the nineteenth century, or as Mr. L. S. Lowry in our own day evolves his remote and formalised men and women standing about improbably in the streets of some northern English city. The detached Gay lived in a world of gentle mockery and beautifully turned phrases:

> In harden'd orbs the school-boy moulds the snow,
> To mark the coachman with a dext'rous throw.
> Why do ye, boys, the kennel's surface spread,
> To tempt with faithless pass the matron's tread?
> How can ye laugh to see the damsel spurn,
> Sink in your frauds, and her green stockings mourn?

How can ye laugh? How can ye not, when Gay's whole manner of describing the incident shows that he is laughing himself, the amused bystander transforming the raw materials of life into his ordered but carefree couplets? Poets such as Gay will nearly always be found contemplating life, already slightly distanced, from a first-floor window, neither loving it nor hating it, but studying it from their own chosen angle of vision, and then devitalising it if necessary, formalising it, polishing it, altering it to suit the sort of poem they are writing and the kind of style they have assumed. *Trivia*, then, is unquestionably artificial; but the artificiality is a way of seeing and ordering the disorderly and haphazard life of the London streets. It is possible here to make a direct comparison with Wordsworth, who recalled, in the seventh book of the *Prelude*, his own early days in London. The memorable passages in that book are all concerned with some isolated figure—the "lovely boy" ("a sort of alien scattered from the clouds") whose fresh innocence contrasts sharply with his sordid environment, the father sitting in the public garden with his sickly child, the blind beggar in whose presence the poet felt "as if admonished from another world". Such passages are far beyond the range of Gay, and can come only from one

> to whom the miseries of the world
> Are misery, and will not let him rest.

But where Wordsworth sets himself to describe a normal street scene the advantage is all with the eighteenth-century poet. On such occasions Wordsworth presents us with the unadorned facts:

> A raree-show is here,
> With children gathered round; another street
> Presents a company of dancing dogs,
> Or dromedary, with an antic pair
> Of monkeys on his back; a minstrel band
> Of Savoyards; or, single and alone,
> An English ballad-singer.

All this Gay would surely have done better. How much more attractive this scene might have been if the dogs had been dancing in the couplets of *Trivia*, and the dromedary and the monkeys had been transformed into something in the nature of heraldic beasts by the delicate artifice of his stylised treatment.

That particular aspect of artificiality, poetic diction, which so exasperated Wordsworth (he called it at various times gaudy, inane, mechanical, false, distorted, adulterated, absurd, vague, glossy, and unfeeling) is less likely to arouse such feelings today. In so far as poetic diction hardened into a set of clichés, that process belongs rather to the middle years of the eighteenth century than to the period covered by this volume. There is little of it in the verse of Prior and Swift, or in the poems of Congreve, Rowe, Lady Winchilsea, Philips and Parnell printed here. It is to be found more frequently in the poems of Gay and Pope, but again, only in those of a certain kind. Epic poetry, which is not represented here, was thought to require a heightened language, and so we find plenty of it in a mock-heroic poem such as *The Rape of the Lock*, or in poems written in a mock-georgic style such as *Trivia* or *The Bowling-Green*. But when Gay writes a song, or when Pope writes a familiar epistle to Teresa Blount, or satirises Addison or Lord Hervey or Timon ("Two Cupids squirt before . . .": "And gaping Tritons spew to wash your face"), the language differs little from that of educated persons of the period. Poetic diction, in fact, cannot be usefully discussed without reference to the kind in which the poet is writing. It should not be forgotten, too, that most eighteenth-century poets had received a prolonged and thorough classical education, and that classical poetry was for them a sort of secondary inspiration, always present at the back of their minds, and often coming to the front in a phrase or a classical allusion.

This volume begins with Congreve and ends with Lord Chesterfield. These two famous names should at least remind us that much of the poetry of the early eighteenth century was characterised by a lively wit and by a delicate and scrupulous care for form and style. Those qualities reach their highest point in Pope, and in selecting poems to represent his work I have deliberately chosen to emphasise his wit, which was brilliant, rather than his morality, which is not perhaps quite so impressive as he liked to think it was, and which was sometimes not much more than a means for setting his wit to work. No doubt he became graver and more deeply concerned about the moral standards of his age as he grew older; but from first to last he was writing, as often as not, in the highest spirits, and with the artist's irrepressible delight in the mastery of his craft. Wit and high spirits are equally apparent in much of the work of Prior, Swift and Gay; and as for the standard of craftsmanship, that too remains remarkably high in the poetry of the period, even when it has comparatively little to work upon. The eighteenth-century poet had more than himself to satisfy: he was about to appear in public, and he knew it; he was conscious of a reader, and was at pains to please him. For twentieth-century readers with a different conception of poetry much of what he wrote may seem to lie somewhere on the undefined border between poetry and rhetoric; but, as Wordsworth once observed, poetry is a word of very disputed meaning, and it would be a pity to allow "the solitary word poetry" to prevent or impede our enjoyment of what is often quite unmistakably great literature.

William Congreve

SONG

THIS song and the lines on Lesbia first appeared in a volume of *Poetical Miscellanies. The Fifth Part*, published by Jacob Tonson in 1704. They are typical examples of the well-turned and balanced verse of the period. They have, too, that amused and fastidious detachment so characteristic of Congreve the writer of comedy. Rowe's "Song on a fine Woman who had a dull Husband" (p. 36) is in the same vein, and as late as 1733 Lord Chesterfield (p. 191) is still carrying on this witty tradition.

> Pious Selinda goes to Pray'rs
>   If I but ask the Favour;
> And yet the tender Fool's in Tears,
>   When she believes I'll leave her.
>
> Wou'd I were free from this Restraint,
>   Or else had Hopes to win her;
> Wou'd she cou'd make of me a Saint,
>   Or I of her a Sinner.

2 *Favour:* sexual intercourse. Cf. Prior, "Chloe Beauty has and Wit", p. 24, l. 10. This word rhymed perfectly with "leave her" in Congreve's day.

LESBIA

> When Lesbia first I saw so heav'nly Fair,
> With Eyes so bright, and with that awful Air,
> I thought my Heart, which durst so high aspire,
> As bold as his, who snatch'd Celestial Fire.
> 5 But soon as e'er the beauteous Idiot spoke,
> Forth from her Coral Lips such Folly broke,
> Like Balm the trickling Nonsense heal'd my Wound,
> And what her Eyes enthral'd, her Tongue unbound.

2 *awful:* awe-inspiring.   4 *his:* i.e. Prometheus.

Matthew Prior

THE SECRETARY

Written at The Hague, in the year 1696

FOR a good part of his life Matthew Prior was in the diplomatic service, first as secretary to the English ambassador at The Hague, and later as secretary in the embassy at Paris. There he played a considerable part in the negotiations which led to the Peace of Utrecht in 1713. Much of his verse was occasional, written in hours snatched from business, but never carelessly and often with a delicate turn. The following verses (not published in his life-time) offer a genial glimpse of the young English diplomat relaxing at the week-end from the boring round of his official duties.

> While with labour assid'ous due pleasure I mix,
> And in one day atone for the bus'ness of six,
> In a little Dutch-chaise on a Saturday night,
> On my left hand my Horace, a Nymph on my right.
> 5　No Memoire to compose, and no Post-Boy to move,
> That on Sunday may hinder the softness of love;
> For her, neither visits, nor parties of tea,
> Nor the long-winded cant of a dull refugee.
> This night and the next shall be hers, shall be mine,
> 10　To good or ill fortune the third we resign:
> Thus scorning the world, and superior to fate,
> I drive on my car, in processional state:
> So with Phia thro' Athens Pysistratus rode,
> Men thought her Minerva, and him a new God.

3 *chaise:* "a carriage of pleasure drawn by one horse" (Johnson, *Dictionary*).

5 *Memoire:* (accented on the second syllable) official report.　*no Post-Boy to move:* i.e. no letters to be dispatched.

8 *refugee:* here probably a Huguenot who had left France owing to the religious persecution after the Revocation of the Edict of Nantes, 1685.

13 *Phia . . . Pysistratus:* Pisistratus played a trick upon the Athenians by passing off a tall, good-looking woman called Phya as the goddess Minerva. Phya then assured the people that she had come down from heaven to establish the rule of Pisistratus in Athens.

15 But why should I stories of Athens rehearse,
Where people knew love, and were partial to verse,
Since none can with justice my pleasures oppose,
In Holland half drowned in int'rest and prose:
By Greece and past ages, what need I be try'd,
20 When the Hague and the present are both at my side;
And is it enough, for the joys of the day,
To think what Anacreon, or Sappho would say,
When good *Vandergoes* and his provident *Vrough*,
As they gaze on my triumph, do freely allow,
25 That search all the province, you'd find no man there is
So bless'd as the *Englischen Heer Secretaris*?

18 *int'rest:* here probably in the sense of "business".   *prose:* i.e. of the
kind mentioned in l. 5.

23 *Vrough:* vrow, wife.

TO A CHILD OF QUALITY OF FIVE YEARS
OLD, THE AUTHOR SUPPOS'D FORTY

THE little girl celebrated in this charming poem was Lady Mary Villiers,
daughter of the first Earl of Jersey. Prior does this sort of thing much better
than Ambrose ("Namby Pamby") Philips, who also addressed several
copies of verses to various high-born little girls. Where Philips is apt to be
merely babyish or mawkish, Prior achieves an affectionate sentiment while
still preserving his wit intact.

Lords, Knights, and Squires, the num'rous Band
    That wear the Fair Miss Mary's Fetters,
Were summon'd, by her high Command,
    To show their Passion by their Letters.

5 My Pen among the rest I took,
    Least those bright Eyes that cannot read
Shou'd dart their kindling Fires, and look
    The Pow'r they have to be obey'd.

6 *Least:* lest.

Nor Quality, nor Reputation,
10   Forbid me yet my Flame to tell,
Dear Five Years old befriends my Passion,
And I may Write 'till she can Spell.

For while she makes her Silk-worms Beds
With all the tender things I swear,
15   Whilst all the House my Passion reads,
In Papers round her Baby's Hair;

She may receive and own my Flame,
For tho' the strictest *Prudes* shou'd know it,
She'll pass for a most virtuous Dame,
20   And I for an unhappy Poet.

Then too, alas, when she shall tear
The Lines some younger Rival sends,
She'll give me leave to Write, I fear,
And we shall still continue Friends.

25   For as our diff'rent Ages move,
'Tis so ordain'd—wou'd Fate but mend it!—
That I shall be past making Love,
When she begins to comprehend it.

16 *Baby's:* doll's.

ANSWER TO CLOE JEALOUS

PRIOR wrote numerous love poems of one sort or another, but Dr. Johnson was of the opinion that his "amorous effusions . . . are not dictated by nature or by passion and have neither gallantry nor tenderness". This is perhaps a fair judgment of most of them, but the first of the two poems that follow certainly does not suffer for being unconventional, and it is written in that easy and familiar style which the poet Cowper thought to be "of all styles the most difficult to succeed in". The second poem has that note of frank but innocuous libertinism which is one of Prior's specialities.

Dear Cloe, how blubber'd is that pretty Face!
    Thy Cheek all on Fire, and Thy Hair all uncurl'd;
Pr'ythee quit this Caprice; and (as Old Falstaf says)
    Let Us e'en talk a little like Folks of This World.

5 How can'st Thou presume, Thou hast leave to destroy
    The Beauties which Venus but lent to Thy keeping?
Those Looks were design'd to inspire Love and Joy:
    More ord'nary Eyes may serve People for weeping.

To be vext at a Trifle or two that I writ,
10   Your Judgment at once, and my Passion You wrong:
You take that for Fact, which will scarce be found Wit:
    Od's Life! must One swear to the Truth of a Song?

What I speak, my fair Cloe, and what I write, shews
    The Diff'rence there is betwixt Nature and Art:
15 I court others in Verse; but I love Thee in Prose:
    And They have my Whimsies; but Thou hast my Heart.

The God of us Verse-men (You know Child) the Sun,
    How after his Journeys He sets up his Rest:
If at Morning o'er Earth 'tis his Fancy to run;
20   At Night he reclines on his Thetis's Breast.

So when I am weary'd with wand'ring all Day,
    To Thee my Delight in the Evening I come:
No Matter what Beauties I saw in my Way,
    They were but my Visits; but Thou art my Home.

3 *as old Falstaf says:* in 2 *Henry IV*, V. iii. 99-101.

17 *the Sun:* Apollo, the sun-god, was also god of poetry.

20 *At Night . . . Breast:* i.e. the sun sets over the sea. (Thetis was one of the sea deities.)

23-4 Prior is probably imitating a passage in Shakespeare, *M.N.D.*, II. ii. 171-2: "My heart with her but as guest-wise sojourn'd,/And now to Helen it is home return'd."

25   Then finish, Dear Cloe, this Pastoral War;
          And let us like Horace and Lydia agree:
     For Thou art a Girl as much brighter than Her,
          As He was a Poet sublimer than Me.

26 *Horace and Lydia:* See Horace, *Odes*, III. ix, where the poet contemplates happily the end of his estrangement from Lydia.

"CHLOE BEAUTY HAS AND WIT"

          Chloe Beauty has and Wit,
          And an Air that is not common;
          Ev'ry Charm does in her meet,
          For to make a handsome Woman.

     5   But we do not only find
          Here, a lovely Face or Feature,
          For she's merciful and kind,
          Beauty's answer'd by good Nature.

          She is always doing good,
    10   Of her Favours never sparing,
          And, as all good Christians shou'd,
          Keeps poor Mortals from despairing.

          Jove the pow'r knew of her Charms,
          And that no man cou'd endure 'em,
    15   So providing 'gainst all harms,
          Gave to her the pow'r to cure 'em.

          And 'twould be a cruel thing,
          When her black Eyes have rais'd desire,
          Shou'd she not her Bucket bring,
    20   And kindly help to quench the Fire.

Isaac Watts

THE DAY OF JUDGMENT
An Ode
Attempted in English Sapphick

ISAAC WATTS (1674-1748), a nonconformist minister, and a prolific writer of verse, is remembered for some of his hymns, and (perhaps more reluctantly) for the moral songs (e.g. "Let dogs delight to bark and bite" and "How doth the little busy bee") that he wrote for children. He was, however, one of the more imaginative poets of the early eighteenth century; and in the following poem he is dealing with a theme, the Last Day, which had a profound appeal for the religious-minded, and which was the occasion for poems—by Pomfret, Edward Young, Watts himself and several others—very different from the conventional religious verse of the period. Watts enjoyed the freedom of the pindaric ode, and in a poem called "The Adventurous Muse" expressed his distaste for the sort of poet who is "correctly dull". His own preference was for the poet who

> Impatient of the reins,
> Pursues an unattempted course,
> Breaks all the critic's iron chains
> And bears to Paradise the raptur'd mind.

In "The Day of Judgment" his decision to write in the sapphic measure imposed some control on his freedom of movement, but not on his imaginative apprehension of his apocalyptic theme.

> When the fierce Northwind with his airy Forces
> Rears up the Baltick to a foaming Fury;
> And the red Lightning with a Storm of Hail comes
>   Rushing amain down,

> 5 How the poor Sailors stand amaz'd and tremble!
> While the hoarse Thunder like a bloody Trumpet
> Roars a loud Onset to the gaping Waters
>   Quick to devour them.

Such shall the Noise be, and the wild Disorder,
10 (If things Eternal may be like these Earthly)
Such the dire Terror when the great Archangel
                        Shakes the Creation;

Tears the strong Pillars of the Vault of Heaven,
Breaks up old Marble the Repose of Princes;
15 Sees the Graves open, and the Bones arising,
                        Flames all around 'em.

Hark the shrill Outcries of the guilty Wretches!
Lively bright Horror and amazing Anguish
Stare thro' their Eye-lids, while the living Worm lies
20   Gnawing within them.

Thoughts like old Vultures prey upon their Heartstrings,
And the smart twinges, when their Eye beholds the
Lofty Judge frowning, and a Flood of Vengeance
                        Rolling afore him.

25 Hopeless Immortals! how they scream and shiver
While Devils push them to the Pit wide yawning
Hideous and gloomy, to receive them headlong
                        Down to the Centre.

Stop here my Fancy: (all away ye horrid
30 Doleful Ideas) come arise to Jesus,
How he sits God-like! and the Saints around him
                        Thron'd, yet adoring!

O may I sit there when he comes Triumphant
Dooming the Nations: then ascend to Glory,
35 While our Hosannahs all along the Passage
                        Shout the Redeemer.

9-13 Watts may be recalling *Paradise Lost*, II. 920-7.
11 *Archangel:* Gabriel.
28 *the Centre:* the centre of the Earth, i.e. Hell.
29 *horrid:* dreadful, terrible.
34 *Dooming:* pronouncing judgment.
35 *the Passage:* the route, the way.

Joseph Addison

"HOW ARE THY SERVANTS BLEST, O LORD!"

SOME of our best-known hymns, including Addison's "The spacious firmament on high" and Isaac Watts's "Our God, our help in ages past", date from the early eighteenth century. This one, which Addison called "a divine ode made by a gentleman upon the conclusion of his travels", first appeared in *The Spectator* of Saturday, September 20, 1712. (Since the Saturday *Spectator* would be read on Sunday it frequently dealt with religious topics.) Addison had set out on a Grand Tour in the late summer of 1699, and did not return to England until the beginning of 1704. On his travels he had met with some of the usual dangers, including a violent storm in the Gulf of Genoa (see ll. 13-32), and the risk of pestilence in Rome, where he "breath'd in tainted Air" (l. 8). In introducing his poem to the readers of *The Spectator*, he observed that there was nothing that affected his imagination so much as the sea. "I cannot see the heavings of this prodigious bulk of waters, even in a calm, without a very pleasing astonishment; but when it is worked up in a tempest, so that the horizon on every side is nothing but foaming billows and floating mountains, it is impossible to describe the agreeable horror that rises from such a prospect. . . . Such an object naturally raises in my thoughts the idea of an Almighty Being, and convinces me of his existence as much as a metaphysical demonstration."

> How are Thy Servants blest, O Lord!
>   How sure is their Defence!
> Eternal Wisdom is their Guide,
>   Their Help Omnipotence.
>
> 5 In foreign Realms, and Lands remote,
>   Supported by Thy Care,
> Through burning Climes I pass'd unhurt,
>   And breath'd in tainted Air.
>
> Thy Mercy sweetned ev'ry Soil,
> 10   Made ev'ry Region please;
> The hoary Alpine Hills it warm'd,
>   And smooth'd the Tyrrhene Seas:

12 *the Tyrrhene Seas:* The Tyrrhene Sea lies between the west coast of Italy and the islands of Corsica, Sardinia and Sicily. After visiting Naples Addison had sailed along the coast to the port of Ostia near Rome.

Think, O my Soul, devoutly think,
    How with affrighted Eyes
15 Thou saw'st the wide extended Deep
    In all its Horrors rise!

Confusion dwelt in ev'ry Face,
    And Fear in ev'ry Heart;
When Waves on Waves, and Gulphs in Gulphs,
20   O'ercame the Pilot's Art.

Yet then from all my Griefs, O Lord,
    Thy Mercy set me free,
Whilst in the Confidence of Pray'r
    My Soul took Hold on Thee:

25 For tho' in dreadful Whirles we hung
    High on the broken Wave,
I knew Thou wert nor slow to hear,
    Nor Impotent to save.

The Storm was laid, the Winds retir'd,
30   Obedient to Thy Will;
The Sea, that roar'd at Thy Command,
    At Thy Command was still.

In Midst of Dangers, Fears and Death,
    Thy Goodness I'll adore,
35 And praise Thee for Thy Mercies past;
    And humbly hope for more.

My Life, if Thou preserv'st my Life,
    Thy Sacrifice shall be;
And Death, if Death must be my Doom,
40   Shall join my Soul to Thee!

Joseph Addison and *Nicholas Amhurst*

THE BOWLING-GREEN

ADDISON was a great admirer of Virgil's *Georgics*, and more especially of
the way in which Virgil could dignify humble occupations by the elegance
of his expression. Virgil, he thought, "breaks the clods, and tosses the dung
about, with an air of gracefulness". One of Addison's own early pieces
was a Latin poem "*Sphaeristerium*", a descriptive account of a game of
bowls in the georgic tradition. This was translated by a young Oxford
undergraduate, Nicholas Amhurst (1697-1742), and published in a volume
of *Poems on Several Occasions*, 1719, from which the text is taken. Amhurst
was shortly afterwards sent down from Oxford for his political activities
(he was at that time an ardent Whig), but later changed sides and became editor of the highly successful Tory journal, *The Craftsman*. In "The
Bowling-Green" he has caught well the mock-heroic diction of the
period, especially its frequent Latinisms, and at the same time done justice
to Addison's Latin original.

> Where smooth and level as the Summer Main,
> A spacious Area opens on the Plain;
> While with descending Dews the Herbage sweats,
> Nor feels the rising Sun's intenser Heats,
> 5 The sharpen'd Scythe prevents the grassy Height,
> And reaps the scanty Harvest of the Night:
> The rolling Stone renews its Morning Round,
> To crush the springing Turf, and sink the knotty Ground.
> And now the polish'd Globes, a num'rous Band,
> 10 Prepar'd for Motion by the Artist's Hand;
> Glitt'ring with Oil, and splendid to the Sight,
> O'er the soft, verdant Surface speed their Flight.
> But least some Bowler should his Cast disown,
> By diff'rent Marks the diff'rent Orbs are known:
> 15 For Gamesters vary; some prefer the Bowl
> That byas'd wheels obliquely to the Goal:

5 *prevents:* forestalls (literally, "comes before").
7 *the rolling stone:* the garden roller.
11 *splendid:* shining.

While others will a diff'rent Choice approve
Of those which in a Line directly move.
The chosen Numbers part on either side,

20   As, or Consent, or doubtful Lots divide;
Each Chief assumes his Arms; when now behold
The Jack exulting o'er the Surface roll'd;
At which their missive Orbs the Bowlers aim,
And who arrives the nearest, wins the Game.

25   The Leader poises in his Hand the Bowl,
And gently launches to the distant Goal:
The current Orb prolongs its circling Course,
Till by Degrees it loses all its Force.
When now another o'er the Level bounds,

30   And Orb succeeding Orb the Block surrounds:
Scatter'd they lie, and barricade the Green,
That scarce a single Bowl can pass between.
When now, with better Skill, and nicer Care,
The dext'rous Youth renews the Wooden War,

35   Beyond the rest his winding Timber flies,
And works insinuating, and wins the Prize.
But if perchance he sees, with Madness stung,
The lagging Wood move impotent along;
If its faint Motion languish on the way,

40   And, short of Length, it press the verdant Lay:
Nimbly he strides behind a-cross the Grass,
And bending hovers o'er the rolling Mass;
Least foul Disgrace should on his Arm redound,
He blames the Rising-Rub and guilty Ground.

20 *doubtful:* uncertain.

22 *exulting:* leaping (a Latinism: *Lat., exultare*).

23 *missive:* sent on their way.

27 *current:* running, rolling.

30 *the Block:* the jack.

36 *insinuating:* in sinuous windings (another Latinism: *insinuare* = to bend, curve).

40 *the verdant Lay:* i.e. lea, the green.

44 *Rising-Rub:* In bowling a "rub" is any obstacle on the green that diverts the bowl from its course.

45   What sudden Laughter echoes o'er the Green,
      When some unlucky, artless Cast is seen;
      When the too pond'rous Lead with stubborn Force
      Allures the Globe from its appointed Course!
      The Bowler chafes, and fruitless Rage ensues,
50   His Body to a Thousand Postures screws:
      He blames he knows not what, with angry Blood,
      He frets, he stamps, and damns th'erroneous Wood:
      Th'erroneous Wood his fruitless Rage disdains,
      And still its former, wayward Course maintains.

55   But if a Bowl, dismiss'd with equal Strength,
      Obtains exactly the intended Length,
      And, nicely passing thro' the crouding Balls,
      Prone on the passive Jack incumbent falls:
      With loud Applause the splitting Heav'ns they rend,
60   And all the Caster and the Cast commend.
      When now the adverse Foe projects around
      His careful Eyes, and marks the ambient Ground:
      And studious the contiguous Globes to part,
      He summons all his Strength and all his Art;
65   Th'extended Vigour of his Nerves applies,
      And rapid from his Arm the brandish'd Engine flies.
      Scarce half so swiftly to the Elëian Goal
      With rival Speed the whirling Chariots roll;
      While the fleet Axle mocks the flagging Wind,
70   And leaves the flying Village far behind.

46 *artless:* clumsy.

47 *Lead:* In Addison's day the bias was given to a bowl by loading it with lead.

52 *erroneous:* wandering aimlessly, i.e. missing the mark.

55 *dismissed:* in its literal sense, "sent away".

62 *ambient:* environing, encompassing.

66 *Engine:* Addison's word here is *"missile" (et missile fortiter urget).* Amhurst uses "engine" in the sense of "weapon of war".

67 *the Elëian Goal:* The Elëi were a people of Elis in the Peloponnesus where the Olympic games were celebrated, and where chariot races therefore took place.

When, if the Wooden Guards, immure the Foe,
And break the Vengeance of the whirling Blow;
If the conflicting Orbs are driv'n around,
And, loosely scatter'd, strew th' Olympic Ground:
75   He chides his Fate, his fervid Spleen boils high,
Calls the Gods false, and Damns the guilty Sky.

But if his Bowl with easy Passage slide,
And with a Clash the wedded Orbs divide;
His Partners shout, the Croud espouse his Cause,
80   And the wide Plain re-murmurs with Applause.

Mean while the Dog-Star burns with sultry Heat,
And ev'ry Limb is drown'd in briny Sweat:
They court the shady Breeze, and cool of Day,
And from their Temples wipe the trickling Drops away.

71 *Wooden Guards:* i.e. bowls which have come to rest in front of the bowl that is nearest the jack and so act as a protection for it.

73 *conflicting:* striking together.

81 *Dog-Star:* Sirius. Cf. *Trivia*, p. 143, l. 146. In ancient times Sirius, the brightest star in the constellation of *Canis Major*, was supposed to cause excessive heat in summer, in the so-called "dog-days" (July 3—August 11).

Anne, Countess of Winchilsea

A NOCTURNAL REVERIE

LADY WINCHILSEA (1661-1720) remained a rather remote figure in the world of eighteenth-century letters. Although she visited London in the winter, and was known to Rowe, Swift and Pope, she lived for the most part a retired life in the country, and her *Miscellany Poems on Several Occasions. Written by a Lady* (1713) did not attract much attention. Her reputation rose considerably in the nineteenth century when Wordsworth showed an interest in her work, more particularly in "A Nocturnal Reverie", but although she wrote other interesting poems, this is easily her best. Her pleased and unforced recording of detailed natural phenomena becomes commoner in the next generation in the work of James Thomson, and later in that of William Cowper.

In such a Night, when every louder Wind
Is to its distant Cavern safe confin'd;
And only gentle Zephyr fans his Wings,
And lonely Philomel, still waking, sings;
5   Or from some Tree, fam'd for the Owl's Delight,
She, hollowing clear, directs the Wand'rer right:
In such a Night, when passing Clouds give place,
Or thinly vail the Heav'ns mysterious Face;
When in some River, overhung with Green,
10   The waving Moon and trembling Leaves are seen;
When freshen'd Grass now bears it self upright,
And makes cool Banks to pleasing Rest invite,
Whence springs the Woodbind, and the Bramble-Rose,
And where the sleepy Cowslip shelter'd grows;
15   Whilst now a paler Hue the Foxglove takes,
Yet checquers still with Red the dusky brakes:
When scatter'd Glow-worms, but in Twilight fine,
Shew trivial Beauties watch their Hour to shine;
Whilst Salisb'ry stands the Test of every Light,
20   In perfect Charms, and perfect Virtue bright:
When Odours, which declin'd repelling Day,
Thro' temp'rate Air uninterrupted stray;
When darken'd Groves their softest Shadows wear,
And falling Waters we distinctly hear;
25   When thro' the Gloom more venerable shows
Some ancient Fabrick, awful in Repose,
While Sunburnt Hills their swarthy Looks conceal,
And swelling Haycocks thicken up the Vale:
When the loos'd Horse now, as his Pasture leads,
30   Comes slowly grazing thro' th' adjoining Meads,
Whose stealing Pace, and lengthen'd Shade we fear,
Till torn up Forage in his Teeth we hear:

3 *Zephyr:* the god of the west wind.
4 *Philomel:* poetic name for the nightingale (after Philomela, who was metamorphosed into a nightingale when attacked by Tereus, the husband of her sister Procne).
13 *Woodbind:* woodbine.   *Bramble-Rose:* dog-rose.
17 *but:* only.

When nibbling Sheep at large pursue their Food,
And unmolested Kine rechew the Cud;
35   When Curlews cry beneath the Village-walls,
And to her straggling Brood the Partridge calls;
Their short-liv'd Jubilee the Creatures keep,
Which but endures, whilst Tyrant-Man do's sleep;
When a sedate Content the Spirit feels,
40   And no fierce Light disturbs, whilst it reveals;
But silent Musings urge the Mind to seek
Something, too high for Syllables to speak;
Till the free Soul to a compos'dness charm'd,
Finding the Elements of Rage disarm'd,
45   O'er all below a solemn Quiet grown,
Joys in th' inferiour World, and thinks it like her Own:
In such a Night let me abroad remain,
Till Morning breaks, and All's confus'd again;
Our Cares, our Toils, our Clamours are renew'd,
50   Or Pleasures, seldom reach'd, again pursu'd.

46 *inferiour:* lower (perhaps in both senses of the word).

Nicholas Rowe

ODE TO VENUS
(Horace, Book IV, Ode i)

NICHOLAS ROWE (1674–1718) succeeded Nahum Tate as poet-laureate and was himself succeeded by Laurence Eusden. In spite of this he was a minor poet of some distinction. His version of Horace's ode to Venus keeps fairly close to the original, and perhaps Rowe's decision to write in a form of free verse (pentameters varied by occasional octosyllabic lines and closing with an alexandrine) enabled him to avoid padding. The text of all three poems included here is from his widow's edition of *The Works*, 1747.

Once more the Queen of Love invades my Breast,
Late, with long Ease, and peaceful Pleasures blest;
Spare, spare the wretch, that still has been thy Slave,
And let my former Service have
5   The Merit to protect me to the Grave.

2 *late:* of late.

Much am I chang'd from what I once have been,
　　When under Cynera the good and fair,
　　With Joy I did thy Fetters wear,
Bless'd in the gentle Sway of an indulgent Queen.
10　Stiff and unequal to the Labor now,
　　With Pain my Neck beneath thy Yoke I bow.
　　Why dost thou urge me still to bear? Oh! why
　　Dost thou not much rather fly
　　To youthful Breasts, to Mirth and Gaiety?
15　Go, bid thy Swans their glossy Wings expand,
　　And swiftly thro' the yielding Air
　　To Damon thee their Goddess bear,
　　Worthy to be thy Slave, and fit for thy Command.
　　Noble, and graceful, witty, gay, and young,
20　Joy in his Heart, Love on his charming Tongue.
　　Skill'd in a Thousand soft prevailing Arts,
　　With wond'rous Force the Youth imparts
　　Thy Pow'r to unexperienc'd Virgins Hearts.
　　Far shall he stretch the Bounds of thy Command;
25　　And if thou shalt his Wishes bless,
　　　Beyond his Rivals with Success,
　　In Gold and Marble shall thy Statues stand.
　　Beneath the sacred Shade of Odel's Wood,
　　Or on the Banks of Ouse's gentle Flood,
30　With od'rous Beams a Temple he shall raise,
　　For ever sacred to thy Praise,
　　Till the fair Stream, and Wood, and Love itself decays.
　　There while rich Incense on thy Altar burns,
　　　Thy Votaries, the Nymphs and Swains,
35　　In melting soft harmonious Strains,
　　Mix'd with the softer Flutes, shall tell their Flames by Turns.
　　As Love and Beauty with the Light are born,
　　So with the Day thy Honors shall return;
　　Some lovely Youth, pair'd with a blushing Maid,

7 *Cynera:* Cinara was a favourite of Horace's.

29 *Ouse's gentle Flood:* Rowe was born in 1674 at Little Barford, a Bedfordshire village on the banks of the Ouse. Odel's Wood (l. 28) is also on the Ouse, about seven miles north-west of Bedford.

40   A Troop of either Sex shall lead,
     And twice the Salian Measures round thy Altar tread.
     Thus with an equal Empire o'er the Light,
         The Queen of Love, and God of Wit,
         Together rise, together sit:
45   But, Goddess, do thou stay, and bless alone the Night.
     There may'st thou reign, while I forget to love;
     No more false Beauty shall my Passion move;
     Nor shall my fond believing Heart be led,
     By mutual Vows and Oaths betray'd,
50   To hope for Truth from the protesting Maid.
     With Love the sprightly Joys of Wine are fled;
         The Roses too shall wither now,
         That us'd to shade and crown my Brow,
     And round my chearful Temples fragrant Odors shed.
55   But tell me, Cynthia, say, bewitching Fair,
     What mean these Sighs? Why steals this falling Tear?
     And when my struggling Thoughts for Passage strove,
     Why did my Tongue refuse to move;
     Tell me can this be any thing but Love?
60   Still with the night my Dreams my Griefs renew,
         Still she is present to my Eyes,
         And still in vain I, as she flies,
     O'er Woods, and Plains, and Seas, the scornful Maid pursue.

41 *Salian Measures:* The *Salii* were priests of Mars. Accompanied by virgins called the *Saliae*, they sang hymns in honour of various gods, including Venus, and also went through the streets together in a measured dance.

43 *God of Wit:* Apollo. Lines 42–6 are an addition of Rowe's.

SONG ON A FINE WOMAN WHO HAD A DULL HUSBAND

When on fair Celia's Eyes I gaze,
    And bless their Light divine;
I stand confounded with Amaze,
    To think on what they shine.

5 On one vile Clod of Earth she seems
  To fix their Influence;
 Which kindles not at those bright Beams,
  Nor wakens into Sense.

 Lost and bewilder'd with the Thought,
10 I cou'd not but complain,
 That Nature's lavish Hand had wrought
  This fairest Work in vain.

 Thus some who have the Stars survey'd,
  Are ignorantly led,
15 To think those glorious Lamps were made
  To light Tom-Fool to Bed.

COLIN'S COMPLAINT

A Song, to the Tune of *Grim King of the Ghosts*

THIS pastoral ballad, written about 1712, was much imitated, and may indeed be said to have given rise to a minor *genre* in eighteenth-century poetry. Rowe's most celebrated imitator was William Shenstone, whose own pastoral ballad, "Ye shepherds so cheerful and gay", was published by Dodsley in the fifth volume of *A Collection of Poems*, 1758. The lilting anapaestic stanza, and, to some extent, the sentimental feeling were new to most readers in Queen Anne's day.

 Despairing beside a clear Stream,
  A Shepherd forsaken was laid;
 And while a false Nymph was his Theme,
  A Willow supported his Head.
5 The Wind that blew over the Plain,
  To his Sighs with a Sigh did reply;
 And the Brook, in return to his Pain,
  Ran mournfully murmuring by.

Alas, silly Swain that I was!
10   Thus sadly complaining he cry'd,
When first I beheld that fair Face,
    'Twere better by far I had dy'd.
She talk'd, and I bless'd the dear Tongue;
    When she smil'd, 'twas a Pleasure too great.
15 I listen'd, and cry'd, when she sung,
    Was Nightingale ever so sweet?

How foolish was I to believe
    She could doat on so lowly a Clown,
Or that her fond Heart would not grieve,
20   To forsake the fine Folk of the Town?
To think that a Beauty so gay,
    So kind and so constant would prove;
Or go clad like our Maidens in Gray,
    Or live in a Cottage on Love.

25 What tho' I have Skill to complain,
    Tho' the Muses my Temples have crown'd;
What tho' when they hear my soft Strain,
    The Virgins sit weeping around.
Ah, Colin, thy Hopes are in vain,
30   Thy Pipe and thy Laurel resign;
Thy false one inclines to a Swain,
    Whose Music is sweeter than thine.

And you, my Companions so dear,
    Who sorrow to see me betray'd,
35 Whatever I suffer, forbear,
    Forbear to accuse the false Maid.
Tho' thro' the wide World I should range,
    'Tis in vain from my Fortune to fly,
'Twas hers to be false and to change,
40   'Tis mine to be constant and die.

If while my hard Fate I sustain,
    In her Breast any Pity is found,
Let her come with the Nymphs of the Plain,
    And see me laid low in the Ground.
45 The last humble Boon that I crave,
    Is to shade me with Cypress and Yew;
And when she looks down on my Grave,
    Let her own that her Shepherd was true.

Then to her new Love let her go,
50   And deck her in golden Array,
Be finest at ev'ry fine Show,
    And frolic it all the long Day;
While Colin, forgotten and gone,
    No more shall be talk'd of, or seen,
55 Unless when beneath the pale Moon,
    His Ghost shall glide over the Green.

Elijah Fenton

AN IMITATION OF THE NINTH ODE OF THE FIRST BOOK OF HORACE

ELIJAH FENTON (1683–1730) edited a collection called *The Oxford and Cambridge Miscellany Poems* (1708), and contributed the two following poems to it. Claudian, a late Latin poet, was born in Alexandria in Egypt. His "Old Man of Verona" was a popular poem in the eighteenth century, and was frequently translated or imitated.

Since the Hills all around do Pennance in Snow,
And Winter's cold Blasts have benumm'd us below;
Since the Rivers chain'd up flow with the same Speed,
As Criminals move to'ards the Psalm they can't read:

4 *the Psalm:* "It is an ancient English custom for the Malefactors to sing a Psalm at their Execution at Tyburn" [Pope, *Dunciad*, I. 41*n*.].

5   Throw whole Oaks at a Time, nay whole Groves on the Fire,
To keep out the Cold, and new Vigour inspire.
Ne'er waste the dull Time in impertinent thinking,
But urge and pursue the grand Bus'ness of drinking.
Come, pierce your old Hogsheads, ne'er stint us in Sherry,
10 For this is the Season to drink and be merry.
That reviv'd by good Liquor, and Billets together,
We may brave the loud storms, and defie the cold Weather.
We'll have no more Bus'ness, but Friend as you love us,
Leave it all to the Care of the good Folks above us.
15 Whilst your Appetite's strong, and good Humour remains,
And active brisk Blood does enliven your Veins,
Improve the sweet Minutes in Scenes of Delight,
Let your Friend have the Day, and your Mistress the Night:
In the dark you may try whether Phyllis is kind,
20 The Night for Intrigues was ever design'd:
Tho' she runs from your Arms, and retires to a Shade,
Some friendly kind sign will betray the coy Maid:
All tremb'ling you'll find the poor bashful Sinner,
Such a Trespass is venial in any Beginner:
25 But remember this Counsel, when once you have met her,
Get a Ring from the Nymph, or something that's better.

7 *impertinent:* out of place, not suitable to the circumstances.
11 *Billets:* firewood.

CLAUDIAN'S "OLD MAN OF VERONA"

Happy the Man who all his Days does pass
In the paternal Cottage of his Race;
Where first his trembling Infant steps he try'd,
Which now supports his Age, and once his Youth employ'd.
5 This was the Cottage his Forefathers knew,
It saw his Birth, shall see his Burial too;
Unequal Fortunes and Ambition's Fate
Are things Experience never taught him yet.
Him to strange Lands no rambling Humour bore,
10 Nor breath'd he ever any Air but of his native Shore.

Free from all anxious Interests of Trade,
No Storms at Sea have e'er disturb'd his Head:
He never Battel's wild Confusions saw,
Nor heard the worse Confusions of the Law.
15   A Stranger to the Town, and Town Employs,
Their dark and crowded Streets, their Stink and Noise;
He a more calm and brighter Sky enjoys.
Nor does the Year by change of Consuls know,
The Year his Fruit's returning Seasons show;
20   Quarters and Months in Nature's Face he sees,
In Flowers the Spring, and Autumn in his Trees.
The whole Day's Shadows in his Homestead drawn,
Point out the hourly Courses of the Sun.
Grown old with him, a Grove adorns his Field,
25   Whose tender setts his Infancy beheld.
Of distant India, Erythraean Shores,
Benacus Lake, Verona's neighb'ring Tow'rs,
(Alike unseen) from common Fame has heard,
Alike believes them, and with like Regard.
30   Yet firm and strong, his Grandchildren admire
The Health and Vigour of their brawny Sire.
The spacious Globe let those that will survey,
This good old Man, content at home to stay,
More happy Years shall know, more Leagues and Countries
    they.

18 *Consuls:* These were elected annually.

25 *setts:* slips or cuttings put into the ground to root.

26 *Erythraean Shores:* When ancient writers refer to the Erythraean sea they meant either the Persian Gulf or the Red Sea.

27 *Benacus Lake:* now known as the Lago di Garda (in northern Italy).

34 *more Leagues:* i.e. more miles travelled.

Jonathan Swift

BAUCIS AND PHILEMON
Imitated, from the Eighth Book of Ovid

THE tale of Baucis and Philemon comes from Ovid's *Metamorphoses*, where the story of how Jove and Mercury rewarded the hospitable peasants is told to convince Perithous, an atheist, of the power of the gods to work miracles. Ovid's tale was translated by Dryden into heroic couplets: Swift's version, in his favourite tetrameter couplets, is not a translation but an imitation in a different key. The kindness of the old couple remains unaffected by Swift's alterations; but the scene has been localised in a humble Kentish cottage, the gods are two hermits, and Swift dwells much more fully on the transformation of the cottage into a church, where the same sort of fancy that was later to find expression in the Voyages to Lilliput and Brobdingnag comes into play. There are, too, a number of characteristic satirical touches that have no equivalent in Ovid, e.g. the bed transformed into pews has retained its old function "by lodging Folks dispos'd to Sleep", and Philemon, carrying out his ecclesiastical duties at the baptismal font, allows his mind to wander to the thought of "whose Sow had farrow'd last". In Ovid the two trees, an oak and a linden, are still to be seen, flourishing presumably to all eternity: in the more realistic Swift they have gone the way of all trees and have been turned to practical uses. Swift, as always, has come back to life as it really is—not harshly or bitterly in this poem, but none the less firmly and unromantically.

> In antient Times, as Story tells,
> The Saints would often leave their Cells,
> And strole about, but hide their Quality,
> To try good People's Hospitality.
>
> 5   It happen'd on a Winter Night,
> As Authors of the Legend write;
> Two Brother Hermits, Saints by Trade,
> Taking their *Tour* in Masquerade;
> Disguis'd in tatter'd Habits, went
> 10 To a small Village down in Kent;
> Where, in the Stroler's Canting Strain,
> They beg'd from Door to Door in vain;
> Try'd ev'ry Tone might Pity win,
> But not a Soul would let them in.

15 Our wand'ring Saints in woeful State,
  Treated at this ungodly Rate,
  Having thro' all the Village pass'd,
  To a small Cottage came at last;
  Where dwelt a good old honest Yeoman,
20 Call'd, in the Neighbourhood, Philemon.
  Who kindly did the Saints invite
  In his Poor Hut to pass the Night;
  And then the Hospitable Sire
  Bid Goody Baucis mend the Fire;
25 While He from out the Chimney took
  A Flitch of Bacon off the Hook;
  And freely from the fattest Side
  Cut out large Slices to be fry'd:
  Then stept aside to fetch 'em Drink,
30 Fill'd a large Jug up to the Brink;
  And saw it fairly twice go round;
  Yet (what is wonderful) they found,
  'Twas still replenished to the Top,
  As if they ne'er had toucht a Drop.
35 The good old Couple was amaz'd,
  And often on each other gaz'd;
  For both were frighted to the Heart,
  And just began to cry;—What ar't!
  Then softly turn'd aside to view,
40 Whether the Lights were burning blue.
  The gentle Pilgrims soon aware on't,
  Told 'em their Calling, and their Errant:
  Good Folks, you need not be afraid,
  We are but Saints, the Hermits said;
45 No Hurt shall come to You, or Yours;
  But, for that Pack of churlish Boors,
  Not fit to live on Christian Ground,
  They and their Houses shall be drown'd:
  Whilst you shall see your Cottage rise,
50 And grow a Church before your Eyes.

---

38 *What ar't*: i.e. What are you?

They scarce had Spoke; when, fair and soft,
The Roof began to mount aloft;
Aloft rose ev'ry Beam and Rafter,
The heavy Wall climb'd slowly after.

55   The Chimney widen'd, and grew higher,
Became a Steeple with a Spire.

The Kettle to the Top was hoist,
And there stood fast'ned to a Joist:
But with the Upside down, to shew
60   Its Inclination for below;
In vain; for a Superior Force
Apply'd at Bottom, stops its Course,
Doom'd ever in Suspence to dwell,
'Tis now no Kettle, but a Bell.

65   A wooden Jack, which had almost
Lost, by Disuse, the Art to Roast,
A sudden Alteration feels,
Increas'd by new Intestine Wheels:
And, what exalts the Wonder more,
70   The Number made the Motion slow'r:
The Flyer, tho't had Leaden Feet,
Turn'd round so quick, you scarce cou'd see't;
But slacken'd by some secret Power,
Now hardly moves an Inch an Hour.
75   The Jack and Chimney near ally'd,
Had never left each other's Side;
The Chimney to a Steeple grown,
The Jack wou'd not be left alone,
But up against the Steeple rear'd,
80   Became a Clock, and still adher'd:

57 *Kettle:* a cauldron, not a tea-kettle. "In the kitchen the name of *pot* is given to the boiler that grows narrower towards the top, and of *kettle* to that which grows wider." (Johnson, *Dictionary*.)

65 *Jack:* a machine for turning a spit. The "flyer" of l. 71 was an appliance for regulating its motion.

And still its Love to Household Cares
By a shrill Voice at Noon declares,
Warning the Cook-maid, not to burn
That Roast-meat which it cannot turn.

85   The Groaning Chair began to crawl
Like an huge Snail along the Wall;
There stuck aloft, in Publick View,
And with small Change, a Pulpit grew.

The Porringers, that in a Row
90   Hung high, and made a glitt'ring Show,
To a less Noble Substance chang'd,
Were now but Leathern Buckets rang'd.

The Ballads pasted on the Wall,
Of Joan of France, and English Moll,
95   Fair Rosamond, and Robin Hood,
The Little Children in the Wood:
Now seem'd to look abundance better,
Improv'd in Picture, Size, and Letter;
And high in Order plac'd, describe
100   The Heraldry of ev'ry Tribe.

A Bedstead of the Antique Mode,
Compact of Timber many a Load,
Such as our Ancestors did use,
Was Metamorphos'd into Pews;
105   Which still their antient Nature keep;
By lodging Folks dispos'd to Sleep.

The Cottage by such Feats as these,
Grown to a Church by just Degrees,
The Hermits then desir'd their Host
110   To ask for what he fancy'd most:
Philemon, having paus'd a while,
Return'd 'em Thanks in homely Stile;

85 *Groaning Chair:* a large bedroom chair, used by women after child-birth.

92 *Leathern Buckets:* used for holding water in case of fire.

Then said; my House is grown so Fine,
Methinks, I still wou'd call it mine:
115 I'm Old, and fain wou'd live at Ease,
Make me the Parson, if you please.

He spoke, and presently he feels
His Grazier's Coat fall down his Heels;
He sees, yet hardly can believe,
120 About each Arm a Pudding-sleeve;
His Wastcoat to a Cassock grew,
And both assum'd a Sable Hue;
But being Old, continu'd just
As Thread-bare, and as full of Dust.
125 His Talk was now of Tythes and Dues,
Cou'd smoak his Pipe, and read the News;
Knew how to preach old Sermons next,
Vampt in the Preface and the Text;
At Christnings well could act his Part,
130 And had the Service all by Heart;
Wish'd Women might have Children fast,
And thought whose Sow had farrow'd last:
Against Dissenters wou'd repine,
And stood up firm for Right Divine:
135 Found his Head fill'd with many a System,
But Classick Authors—he ne'er miss'd 'em.

Thus having furbish'd up a Parson,
Dame Baucis next, they play'd their Farce on:
Instead of Home-spun Coifs were seen
140 Good Pinners edg'd with Colberteen:

120 *Pudding-sleeve:* a bulging sleeve pulled in at the wrist.

132 *whose Sow has farrow'd:* As parson, Philemon was entitled to a tithe-pig.

134 *Right Divine:* i.e. the divine right of kings, asserted by the High Church party.

139 *Coifs:* close-fitting caps covering the head.

140 *Pinners:* coifs with two long flaps, worn by upper-class women. *Colberteen:* a kind of lace.

Her Petticoat transform'd apace,
Became Black Sattin, Flounc'd with Lace.
Plain *Goody* would no longer down,
'Twas *Madam*, in her Grogram Gown.
145 Philemon was in great Surprize,
And hardly could believe his Eyes,
Amaz'd to see Her look so Prim,
And she admir'd as much at Him.

Thus, happy in their Change of Life,
150 Were several Years this Man and Wife,
When on a Day, which prov'd their last,
Discoursing on old Stories past,
They went by chance, amidst their Talk,
To the Church-yard, to take a Walk;
155 When Baucis hastily cry'd out;
My Dear, I see your Forehead sprout:
Sprout, quoth the Man, What's this you tell us?
I hope you don't believe me Jealous:
But yet, methinks, I feel it true—
160 And re'ly, Yours is budding too—
Nay,—now I cannot stir my Foot:
It feels as if 'twere taking Root.

Description would but tire my Muse:
In short, they both were turn'd to Yews.
165 Old Good-man Dobson of the Green
Remembers he the Trees has seen;
He'll talk of them from Noon till Night,
And goes with Folks to shew the Sight:
On Sundays, after Ev'ning Prayer,
170 He gathers all the Parish there:
Points out the Place of either Yew;
Here Baucis, there Philemon grew.

143 *down:* i.e. go down with her.
144 *Grogram:* a fabric of coarse silk.
148 *admir'd:* wondered.
158 *Jealous:* suspicious that he was a cuckold.

Till once, a Parson of our Town,
To mend his Barn, cut Baucis down;
175   At which, 'tis hard to be believ'd,
How much the other Tree was griev'd,
Grew Scrubby, dy'd a-top, was stunted:
So, the next Parson stub'd and burnt it.

178 *stub'd:* grubbed up by the roots.

A DESCRIPTION OF THE MORNING

THE two following pieces were written when Swift, then an Irish clergy-man, was on a prolonged visit to London. They were published in *The Tatler*, April 30, 1709 and October 17, 1710. Swift himself thought the "Shower" much the better of the two, but both poems show the same dis-enchanted, anti-romantic attitude which appears in so much of his writing. In place of the usual clichés about "the rosy-fingered morn", etc., Swift takes a hard look at the world around him; and it is not (to take one obvious contrast) a flock of Arcadian sheep that he sees returning to the fold, but the prisoners released illegally by the warder the night before and now sneaking back to jail. Introducing the first poem to the readers of *The Tatler*, Steele rightly observed that the author "never forms fields, or nymphs, or groves where they are not, but makes the incidents just as they really appear". When the second poem was reprinted in 1727 it was said to be an imitation of Virgil's *Georgics*. The weather signs in the opening lines are in the georgic tradition, and so is the occasionally inflated language ("contiguous Drops", "the South rising with dabbled Wings", etc.); but the poem everywhere hovers intentionally between the distantly heroic and the immediately actual, between the literary and the colloquial, the traditional and the unconventional.

Now hardly here and there an Hackney-Coach
Appearing, show'd the Ruddy Morns Approach.
Now Betty from her Masters Bed had flown,
And softly stole to discompose her own.
5   The Slipshod Prentice from his Masters Door,
Had par'd the Dirt, and Sprinkled round the Floor.
Now Moll had whirl'd her Mop with dext'rous Airs,
Prepar'd to Scrub the Entry and the Stairs.

6 *Sprinkled:* i.e. sprinkled water to lay the dust.

The Youth with Broomy Stumps began to trace
10 The Kennel-Edge, where Wheels had worn the Place.
The Smallcoal-Man was heard with Cadence deep,
'Till drown'd in Shriller Notes of Chimney-Sweep,
Duns at his Lordships Gate began to meet,
And Brickdust Moll had Scream'd through half the Street.
15 The Turnkey now his Flock returning sees,
Duly let out a Nights to Steal for Fees.
The watchful Bailiffs take their silent Stands,
And School-Boys lag with Satchels in their Hands.

10 *Kennel:* street-gutter.

11 *Smallcoal:* household coal.

14 *Brickdust:* used for scouring pots, knives, etc.

15-16 *The Turnkey . . . Fees:* By paying certain "fees" to the gaoler, prisoners could obtain various privileges. The one mentioned here was, of course, quite irregular and illegal.

17 *Bailiffs:* officers of justice waiting to serve a writ or warrant on some individual (e.g. for debt).

A DESCRIPTION OF A CITY SHOWER

Careful Observers may foretel the Hour
(By sure Prognosticks) when to dread a Show'r:
While Rain depends, the pensive Cat gives o'er
Her Frolicks, and pursues her Tail no more.
5 Returning Home at Night, you'll find the Sink
Strike your offended Sense with double Stink.
If you be wise, then go not far to Dine,
You'll spend in Coach-hire more than save in Wine.
A coming Show'r your shooting Corns presage,
10 Old Aches throb, your hollow Tooth will rage.
Sauntring in Coffee-house is Dulman seen;
He damns the Climate, and complains of Spleen.

3 *depends:* impends, is coming.

10 *aches:* pronounced "aitches".

12 *Spleen:* hypochondria, a prevalent malady in the eighteenth century.

Mean while the South rising with dabbled Wings,
A Sable Cloud a-thwart the Welkin flings,
15 That swill'd more Liquor than it could contain,
And like a Drunkard gives it up again.
Brisk Susan whips her Linen from the Rope,
While the first drizzling Show'r is born aslope,
Such is that Sprinkling which some careless Quean
20 Flirts on you from her Mop, but not so clean.
You fly, invoke the Gods; then turning, stop
To rail; she singing, still whirls on her Mop.
Not yet, the Dust had shun'd th'unequal Strife,
But aided by the Wind, fought still for Life;
25 And wafted with its Foe by violent Gust,
'Twas doubtful which was Rain, and which was Dust.
Ah! where must needy Poet seek for Aid,
When Dust and Rain at once his Coat invade?
His only Coat, where Dust confus'd with Rain,
30 Roughen the Nap, and leave a mingled Stain.

Now in contiguous Drops the Flood comes down,
Threat'ning with Deluge this Devoted Town.
To Shops in Crouds the daggled Females fly,
Pretend to cheapen Goods, but nothing buy.
35 The Templer spruce, while ev'ry Spout's a-broach,
Stays till 'tis fair, yet seems to call a Coach.
The tuck'd-up Sempstress walks with hasty Strides,
While Streams run down her oil'd Umbrella's Sides.
Here various Kinds by various Fortunes led,
40 Commence Acquaintance underneath a Shed.
Triumphant Tories, and desponding Whigs,
Forget their Fewds, and join to save their Wigs.

---

13 *dabbled:* splashed, soiled.   **19** *Quean:* wench.

32 *Devoted:* doomed.   **33** *daggled:* splashed with rain and mud.

34 *cheapen:* ask the price of.

41 *Triumphant Tories . . . desponding Whigs:* Just before this poem was written the Whig ministers had fallen from power and had been replaced by Tories.

Box'd in a Chair the Beau impatient sits,
While Spouts run clatt'ring o'er the Roof by Fits
45 And ever and anon with frightful Din
The Leather sounds, he trembles from within.
So when Troy Chair-men bore the Wooden Steed,
Pregnant with Greeks, impatient to be freed,
(Those Bully Greeks, who, as the Moderns do,
50 Instead of paying Chair-men, run them thro')
Laoco'n struck the Outside with his Spear,
And each imprison'd Hero quak'd for Fear.

Now from all Parts the swelling Kennels flow,
And bear their Trophies with them as they go:
55 Filth of all Hues and Odours seem to tell
What Street they sail'd from, by their Sight and Smell.
They, as each Torrent drives, with rapid Force
From Smithfield, or St. Pulchre's shape their Course,
And in huge Confluent join at Snow-Hill Ridge,
60 Fall from the Conduit prone to Holborn-Bridge.
Sweepings from Butchers Stalls, Dung, Guts, and Blood,
Drown'd Puppies, stinking Sprats, all drench'd in Mud,
Dead Cats and Turnip-Tops come tumbling down the Flood.

43 *Chair:* i.e. a sedan chair which had a roof made of leather.

47 *the Wooden Steed:* For the story of the Wooden Horse and Laocöon, the Trojan priest, see *Aeneid*, ii.

58-60 *From Smithfield . . . to Holborn-Bridge:* On a wet day the garbage from Smithfield Market and the less specialised dirt from the neighbourhood of St. Sepulchre's Church would be carried westward along the 'kennels' until it came to the top of Snow Hill, which dropped sharply to the Fleet River. From Snow Hill all this muck would naturally rush downwards to the point where Holborn Bridge spanned the Fleetditch.

61-3 A note to this poem in Faulkner's edition of *The Works*, 1735, reads: "The three last lines were intended against that licentious Manner of modern Poets, in making three Rhimes together, which they call *Triplets*; and the last of the three was two or sometimes more Syllables longer, called an *Alexandrian*." In this, as in many other matters, Swift was a strict disciplinarian.

VERSES ON THE DEATH OF DR. SWIFT

Occasioned by reading a Maxim in Rochefoulcault

Dans l'adversité de nos meilleurs amis nous trouvons quelque chose qui ne nous deplaist pas.

THIS poem was written in 1731, but not published until 1739. Beginning with La Rochefoucauld's maxim that "in the adversity of our best friends we find something that does not displease us", Swift proceeds to develop this theme, passes on to a consideration of how quickly the dead are forgotten, and then (307 ff.) draws his own character for us and gives an account of his most important activities. If this last part of the poem is not quite so impartial as Swift himself suggests, it is not far from the truth. The situation of a man writing his own obituary had all those ironical possibilities that Swift could be counted upon to exploit. More profoundly, his realisation that "we shall all die alone" and that other people are too busy attending to their own lives to spare much thought for the dying or the dead gives a sardonic edge to his account of the way in which the news of his last illness and death are received. The level voice and controlled feeling of Swift give power to a poem which is all the more moving because it is written with such apparent indifference and lack of emotion. The text is that of Sir Harold Williams' recension of Faulkner's edition of 1739. Some of the notes that Swift provided are reprinted here; others are paraphrased.

> As Rochefoulcault his Maxims drew
> From Nature, I believe 'em true:
> They argue no corrupted Mind
> In him; the Fault is in Mankind.

> 5   This Maxim more than all the rest
> Is thought too base for human Breast;
> "In all Distresses of our Friends
> We first consult our private Ends,
> While Nature kindly bent to ease us,
> 10   Points out some Circumstance to please us."

> If this perhaps your Patience move
> Let Reason and Experience prove.

12 *prove:* put it to the test.

We all behold with envious Eyes,
Our *Equal* rais'd above our *Size*;
15 Who wou'd not at a crowded Show,
Stand high himself, keep others low?
I love my Friend as well as you,
But would not have him stop my View;
Then let him have the higher Post;
20 I ask but for an Inch at most.

If in a Battle you should find,
One, whom you love of all Mankind,
Had some heroick Action done,
A Champion kill'd, or Trophy won;
25 Rather than thus be over-topt,
Would you not wish his Lawrels cropt?

Dear honest Ned is in the Gout,
Lies rackt with Pain, and you without:
How patiently you hear him groan!
30 How glad the Case is not your own!

What Poet would not grieve to see,
His Brethren write as well as he?
But rather than they should excel,
He'd wish his Rivals all in Hell.

35 Her End when Emulation misses,
She turns to Envy, Stings and Hisses:
The strongest Friendship yields to Pride,
Unless the Odds be on our Side.

Vain human Kind! Fantastick Race!
40 Thy various Follies, who can trace?
Self-love, Ambition, Envy, Pride,
Their Empire in our Hearts divide:
Give others Riches, Power, and Station,
'Tis all on me an Usurpation.

45 I have no Title to aspire;
    Yet, when you sink, I seem the higher.
    In Pope, I cannot read a Line,
    But with a Sigh, I wish it mine:
    When he can in one Couplet fix
50 More Sense than I can do in Six:
    It gives me such a jealous Fit,
    I cry, "Pox take him, and his Wit."

    Why must I be outdone by Gay,
    In my own hum'rous biting Way?

55   Arbuthnot is no more my Friend,
    Who dares to Irony pretend;
    Which I was born to introduce,
    Refin'd it first, and shew'd its Use.

    St. John, as well as Pultney knows,
60 That I had some repute for Prose;
    And till they drove me out of Date,
    Could maul a Minister of State:
    If they have mortify'd my Pride,
    And made me throw my Pen aside;
65 If with such Talents Heav'n hath blest 'em
    Have I not Reason to detest 'em?

    To all my Foes, dear Fortune, send
    Thy Gifts, but never to my Friend:
    I tamely can endure the first,
70 But, this with Envy makes me burst.

55 *Arbuthnot:* Dr. John Arbuthnot (1667-1735) had shown his irony in *The History of John Bull, The Art of Political Lying*, and elsewhere.

56 *pretend:* lay claim.

59 *St. John . . . Pultney:* Henry St. John, Viscount Bolingbroke, and William Pultney, later Earl of Bath. Both men were at this time in opposition and "mauling" Sir Robert Walpole, the chief minister, in *The Craftsman.*

Thus much may serve by way of Proem,
Proceed we therefore to our Poem.

The Time is not remote, when I
Must by the Course of Nature dye:
75 When I foresee my special Friends,
Will try to find their private Ends:
Tho' it is hardly understood,
Which way my Death can do them good;
Yet thus methinks, I hear 'em speak;
80 "See how the Dean begins to break:
Poor Gentleman, he droops apace,
You plainly find it in his Face:
That old Vertigo in his Head,
Will never leave him, till he's dead:
85 Besides his Memory decays,
He recollects not what he says;
He cannot call his Friends to Mind;
Forgets the Place where last he din'd:
Plyes you with Stories o'er and o'er,
90 He told them fifty Times before.
How does he fancy we can sit,
To hear his out-of-fashion'd Wit?
But he takes up with younger Fokes,
Who for his Wine will bear his Jokes:
95 Faith, he must make his Stories shorter,
Or change his Comrades once a Quarter:
In half the Time, he talks them round;
There must another Sett be found.

"For Poetry, he's past his Prime,
100 He takes an Hour to find a Rhime:
His Fire is out, his Wit decay'd,
His Fancy sunk, his Muse a Jade.
I'd have him throw away his Pen:
But there's no talking to some Men."

76 *find their private Ends:* take what advantage of the situation they can.
80 *break:* fail (usually of bankrupts).
83 *Vertigo:* Swift suffered for many years from attacks of giddiness.

105   And then their Tenderness appears,
       By adding largely to my Years:
       "He's older than he would be reckon'd,
       And well remembers Charles the Second.

       "He hardly drinks a Pint of Wine;
110   And that, I doubt, is no good Sign.
       His Stomach too begins to fail:
       Last Year we thought him strong and hale;
       But now, he's quite another Thing;
       I wish he may hold out till Spring."

115   Then hug themselves, and reason thus;
       "It is not yet so bad with us."

       In such a Case they talk in Tropes,
       And by their Fears express their Hopes:
       Some great Misfortune to portend,
120   No Enemy can match a Friend;
       With all the Kindness they profess,
       The Merit of a lucky Guess,
       (When daily Howd'y's come of Course,
       And Servants answer; *Worse and Worse*)
125   Wou'd please 'em better than to tell,
       That, God be prais'd, the Dean is well.
       Then he who prophecy'd the best,
       Approves his Foresight to the rest:
       "You know, I always fear'd the worst,
130   And often told you so at first:"
       He'd rather chuse that I should dye,
       Than his Prediction prove a Lye.
       Not one foretels I shall recover;
       But all agree to give me over.

108 *Charles the Second:* Swift was seventeen when Charles II died.
123 *Howd'y's:* enquiries about someone's health, usually given to foot-
men to deliver.

135   Yet shou'd some Neighbour feel a Pain,
 Just in the Parts, where I complain;
 How many a Message would he send?
 What hearty Prayers that I should mend?
 Enquire what Regimen I kept;
140   What gave me Ease, and how I slept?
 And more lament, when I was dead,
 Than all the Sniv'llers round my Bed.

 My good Companions, never fear,
 For though you may mistake a Year;
145   Though your Prognosticks run too fast,
 They must be verify'd at last.

 Behold the fatal Day arrive!
 "How is the Dean?"—"He's just alive."
 Now the departing Prayer is read:
150   "He hardly breathes. The Dean is dead."
 Before the Passing-Bell begun,
 The News thro' half the Town has run.
 "O, may we all for Death prepare!
 What has he left? And who's his Heir?"
155   "I know no more than what the News is,
 'Tis all bequeath'd to publick Uses."
 "To publick Use! A perfect Whim!
 What had the Publick done for him!
 Meer Envy, Avarice, and Pride!
160   He gave it all:—But first he dy'd.
 And had the Dean, in all the Nation,
 No worthy Friend, no poor Relation?
 So ready to do Strangers good,
 Forgetting his own Flesh and Blood?"

165   Now Grub-Street Wits are all employ'd;
 With Elegies, the Town is cloy'd:

156 *publick Uses:* cf. ll. 479-80.

Some Paragraph in ev'ry Paper,
To *curse* the *Dean*, or *bless* the *Drapier*.

The Doctors tender of their Fame,
170 Wisely on me lay all the Blame:
"We must confess his Case was nice;
But he would never take Advice:
Had he been rul'd, for ought appears,
He might have liv'd these Twenty Years:
175 For when we open'd him we found,
That all his vital Parts were sound."

From Dublin soon to London spread,
'Tis told at Court, the Dean is dead.

Kind Lady Suffolk in the Spleen,
180 Runs laughing up to tell the Queen.
The Queen, so Gracious, Mild, and Good,
Cries, "Is he gone? 'Tis time he shou'd.
He's dead you say; why let him rot;
I'm glad the Medals were forgot.

168 *the Dean . . . the Drapier:* "The Author imagines that the Scriblers of the prevailing Party [i.e. the Whigs], which he always opposed, will libel him after his Death; but that others will remember him with Gratitude, who consider the Service he had done to Ireland, under the Name of M. B. Drapier, by utterly defeating the destructive Project of Wood's Half-pence, in five Letters to the People of Ireland, at that Time read universally, and convincing every Reader." [Swift.] Swift's *Drapier's Letters* written against William Wood, who had been given a patent to coin Irish halfpennies and farthings, began to appear in 1724.

171 *nice:* calling for delicate treatment.

179 *Lady Suffolk:* Mrs. Howard, afterwards Countess of Suffolk, was a friend of Pope and Gay, but Swift took a dislike to her. She was a Lady of the Bedchamber to the Queen, and mistress of George II.

184 *the Medals:* Queen Caroline had promised Swift some medals in exchange for some material woven in Ireland, but she failed to keep her promise, and he never forgave her. In a long indignant note to this passage he tells how she "forgot them, or thought them too dear".

185   I promis'd them, I own; but when?
       I only was the Princess then;
       But now as Consort of the King,
       You know 'tis quite a different Thing."

       Now, Chartres at Sir Robert's Levee,
190   Tells, with a Sneer, the Tidings heavy:
       "Why, is he dead without his Shoes?"
       (Cries Bob) "I'm Sorry for the News;
       Oh, were the Wretch but living still,
       And in his Place my good Friend Will;
195   Or, had a Mitre on his Head
       Provided Bolingbroke were dead."

       Now Curl his Shop from Rubbish drains;
       Three genuine Tomes of Swift's Remains.
       And then to make them pass the glibber,
200   Revis'd by Tibbalds, Moore, and Cibber.
       He'll treat me as he does my Betters.
       Publish my Will, my Life, my Letters.
       Revive the Libels born to dye;
       Which Pope must bear, as well as I.

189 *Chartres:* Francis Charteris (1675-1732), a notorious profligate. In a note Swift explains that "he was Tryed . . . for a Rape, and came off by sacrificing a great Part of his Fortune . . ."   *Sir Robert's Levee:* Sir Robert Walpole was the chief minister of the Whig government. His "levee" was a reception for visitors held in the morning.

194 *Will:* William Pulteney. Cf. l. 59.

197 *Curl:* Edmund Curll, an enterprising and unscrupulous publisher. He was ridiculed in Pope's *Dunciad.* "He published three Volumes all charged on the Dean, who never writ three Pages of them. . . ." [Swift.]

200 *Tibbalds, Moore, and Cibber:* Lewis Theobald, dramatist and editor of Shakespeare; James Moore Smythe, a poetaster; and Colley Cibber, actor, dramatist and poet-laureate—all three satirised in *The Dunciad* and elsewhere.

202 *Publish my Will:* "Curl is notoriously infamous for publishing the Lives, Letters, and last Wills and Testaments of the Nobility and Ministers of State, as well as of all the Rogues who are hanged at Tyburn. . . ." [Swift.]

205   Here shift the Scene, to represent
How those I love, my Death lament.
Poor Pope will grieve a Month; and Gay
A Week; and Arbuthnott a Day.

St. John himself will scarce forbear,
210 To bite his Pen, and drop a Tear.
The rest will give a Shrug and cry,
"I'm sorry; but we all must dye."
Indifference clad in Wisdom's Guise,
All Fortitude of Mind supplies:
215 For how can stony Bowels melt,
In those who never Pity felt;
When *We* are lash'd, *They* kiss the Rod;
Resigning to the Will of God.

The Fools, my Juniors by a Year,
220 Are tortur'd with Suspence and Fear.
Who wisely thought my Age a Screen,
When Death approach'd to stand between:
The Screen remov'd, their Hearts are trembling,
They mourn for me without dissembling.

225   My female Friends, whose tender Hearts
Have better learn'd to act their Parts,
Receive the News in *doleful Dumps*,
"The Dean is dead, (*and what is Trumps?*)
Then Lord have Mercy on his Soul.
230 (Ladies I'll venture for the *Vole*.)
Six Deans they say must bear the Pall.
(I wish I knew what *King* to call.)
Madam, your Husband will attend
The Funeral of so good a Friend."

227 *doleful Dumps*: a phrase from the old ballad of "Chevy Chase".
230 *the Vole*: a term in the game of "quadrille" for winning all the tricks.
Quadrille had succeeded ombre (cf. *The Rape of the Lock*) as the fashionable
card game.

235 "No Madam, 'tis a shocking Sight,
      And he's engag'd To-morrow Night!
      My Lady Club wou'd take it ill,
      If he shou'd fail her at Quadrill.
      He lov'd the Dean. (*I lead a Heart.*)
240 But dearest Friends, they say, must part.
      His Time was come, he ran his Race;
      We hope he's in a better Place."

         Why do we grieve that Friends should dye?
      No Loss more easy to supply.
245 One Year is past; a different Scene;
      No further mention of the Dean;
      Who now, alas, no more is mist,
      Than if he never did exist.
      Where's now this Fav'rite of Apollo?
250 Departed: *and his Works must follow:*
      Must undergo the common Fate;
      His Kind of Wit is out of Date.
      Some Country Squire to Lintot goes,
      Enquires for Swift in Verse and Prose:
255 Says Lintot, "I have heard the Name:
      He dy'd a Year ago."—"The same."
      He searcheth all his Shop in vain;
      "Sir you may find them in Duck-lane:
      I sent them with a Load of Books,
260 Last Monday to the Pastry-cooks.
      To fancy they cou'd live a Year!
      I find you're but a Stranger here.
      The Dean was famous in his Time;
      And had a Kind of Knack at Rhyme:
265 His way of Writing now is past;
      The Town hath got a better Taste:

255 *Lintot:* Bernard Lintot, one of the leading booksellers and publishers.

258 *Duck-lane:* a street near Smithfield in which many second-hand booksellers had their stalls.

260 *Pastry-cooks:* The paper from old books was sometimes used to line pie-dishes.

I keep no antiquated Stuff;
But, spick and span I have enough.
Pray, do but give me leave to shew 'em;
270 Here's Colley Cibber's Birth-day Poem.
This Ode you never yet have seen,
By Stephen Duck, upon the Queen.
Then, here's a Letter finely penn'd
Against the *Craftsman* and his Friend;
275 It clearly shews that all Reflection
On Ministers, is disaffection.
Next, here's Sir Robert's Vindication,
And Mr. Henly's last Oration:
The Hawkers have not got 'em yet,
280 Your Honour please to buy a Set?

"Here's Wolston's Tracts, the twelfth Edition;
'Tis read by ev'ry Politician:
The Country Members, when in Town,
To all their Boroughs send them down:

270 *Birth-day Poem:* The poet-laureate was expected to produce an annual ode for the King's birthday.

272 *Stephen Duck:* a Wiltshire agricultural labourer who wrote poetry. The wits ridiculed him, but he was patronised by Queen Caroline—a sufficient reason for Swift's introducing him here.

274 *the Craftsman: The Craftsman*, which had been running since 1726, was the chief anti-Whig weekly.   *his Friend:* i.e. Swift's friend, Bolingbroke.

277 *Sir Robert's Vindication:* "Walpole hires a Set of Party Scriblers, who do nothing else but write in his Defence." [Swift.]

278 *Henly's last Oration:* The Rev. John Henley, a clergyman who took a short cut to notoriety by opening what he called an oratory in Newport Market. "There, at set Times, he delivereth strange Speeches compiled by himself and his Associates, who share the Profit with him: Every Hearer pays a Shilling each Day for Admittance." [Swift.] See *The Dunciad*, Book III. Henley was probably not certifiable, but he was certainly eccentric.

281 *Wolston's Tracts:* Thomas Woolston (1670–1733) published six *Discourses on the Miracles of our Saviour*, 1729, for which he was found guilty of blasphemy. In attacking Woolston Swift was attacking Queen Caroline, who was notoriously sympathetic to freethinkers.

285 You never met a Thing so smart;
  The Courtiers have them all by Heart:
  Those Maids of Honour (who can read)
  Are taught to use them for their Creed.
  The Rev'rend Author's good Intention,
290 Hath been rewarded with a Pension:
  He doth an Honour to his Gown,
  By bravely running Priest-craft down:
  He shews, as sure as God's in Gloc'ster,
  That Jesus was a Grand Impostor:
295 That all his Miracles were Cheats,
  Perform'd as Juglers do their Feats:
  The Church had never such a Writer:
  A Shame, he hath not got a Mitre!"

  Suppose me dead; and then suppose
300 A Club assembled at the *Rose*;
  Where from Discourse of this and that,
  I grow the Subject of their Chat:
  And, while they toss my Name about,
  With Favour some, and some without;
305 One quite indiff'rent in the Cause,
  My Character impartial draws:

  "The Dean, if we believe Report,
  Was never ill receiv'd at Court:
  As for his Works in Verse and Prose,
310 I own my self no Judge of those:
  Nor, can I tell what Criticks thought 'em;
  But, this I know, all People bought 'em;
  As with a moral View design'd
  To cure the Vices of Mankind:
315 His Vein, ironically grave,
  Expos'd the Fool, and lash'd the Knave:

293 *as sure as God's in Gloc'ster:* a proverbial expression.
300 *the Rose:* a celebrated tavern near Drury Lane Theatre.

To steal a Hint was never known,
But what he writ was all his own.

"He never thought an Honour done him,
320 Because a Duke was proud to own him:
Would rather slip aside, and chuse
To talk with Wits in dirty Shoes:
Despis'd the Fools with Stars and Garters,
So often seen caressing Chartres:
325 He never courted Men in Station,
Nor Persons had in Admiration;
Of no Man's Greatness was afraid,
Because he sought for no Man's Aid.
Though trusted long in great Affairs,
330 He gave himself no haughty Airs:
Without regarding private Ends,
Spent all his Credit for his Friends:
And only chose the Wise and Good;
No Flatt'rers; no Allies in Blood;
335 But succour'd Virtue in Distress,
And seldom fail'd of good Success;
As Numbers in their Hearts must own,
Who, but for him, had been unknown.

"With Princes kept a due Decorum,
340 But never stood in Awe before 'em:
He follow'd David's Lesson just,
In Princes never put thy Trust.
And, would you make him truly sower;
Provoke him with *a slave in Power:*
345 The Irish Senate, if you nam'd,
With what Impatience he declaim'd!
Fair LIBERTY was all his Cry;
For her he stood prepar'd to die;

317-18 A reminiscence of two lines of Sir John Denham, "On Mr. Abraham Cowley", ll. 29-30.

326 *Persons:* personages, people of importance.

342 *In Princes . . . trust:* Psalms, cxlvi, 3.

For her he boldly stood alone;
350 For her he oft expos'd his own.
Two Kingdoms, just as Faction led,
Had set a Price upon his Head;
But, not a Traytor cou'd be found,
To Sell him for Six Hundred Pound.

355   "Had he but spar'd his Tongue and Pen,
He might have rose like other Men;
But, Power was never in his Thought;
And, Wealth he valu'd not a Groat:
Ingratitude he often found,
360 And pity'd those who meant the Wound:
But, kept the Tenor of his Mind,
To merit well of human Kind:
Nor made a Sacrifice of those
Who still were true, to please his Foes.
365 He labour'd many a fruitless Hour
To reconcile his Friends in Power;
Saw Mischief by a Faction brewing,
While they pursu'd each others Ruin.
But, finding vain was all his Care,
370 He left the Court in meer Despair.

        "And, oh! how short are human Schemes!
Here ended all our golden Dreams.
What St. John's Skill in State Affairs,
What Ormond's *Valour*, Oxford's Cares,

352 *a Price upon his Head:* Swift recalls in a note how in 1713 a reward of
£300 was offered for information leading to the arrest of the author of
The Public Spirit of the Whigs (one of his pamphlets), and how again in 1724
the Lord Lieutenant of Ireland offered the same award for anyone who could
discover the author of the fourth of the *Drapier's Letters*.

366 *To reconcile his Friends:* In the closing months of Queen Anne's reign
Bolingbroke and the Earl of Oxford, then the two chief ministers of the
Tory government, quarrelled. After trying in vain to reconcile them,
Swift retired, first to a Berkshire rectory, and eventually to his deanery in
Dublin.

374 *Ormond's Valour:* James Butler, Duke of Ormonde, was appointed

375   To save their sinking Country lent,
Was all destroy'd by one Event.
Too soon that precious Life was ended,
On which alone, our Weal depended.
When up a dangerous Faction starts,

380   With Wrath and Vengeance in their Hearts:
By solemn League and Cov'nant bound,
To ruin, slaughter, and confound;
To turn Religion to a Fable,
And make the Government a *Babel:*

385   Pervert the Law, disgrace the Gown,
Corrupt the Senate, rob the Crown;
To sacrifice old England's Glory,
And make her infamous in Story.
When such a Tempest shook the Land,

390   How could unguarded Virtue stand?

"With Horror, Grief, Despair the Dean
Beheld the dire destructive Scene:
His Friends in Exile, or the Tower,
Himself within the Frown of Power;

Commander-in-Chief when the Tories dismissed the Duke of Marl-borough in 1713.

377 *that precious Life was ended:* "In the Height of the Quarrel between the Ministers, the Queen died." [Swift.] Bolingbroke, who had ousted Oxford, had not time to deal with the new situation, and was swept aside by the Whigs.

379 *a dangerous Faction:* i.e. the Whig party.

381 *solemn League and Cov'nant:* a pact signed by the English and Scottish parliaments, then predominantly presbyterian, in 1643. Swift uses the phrase here to taunt the Whigs, who were in general Low Church.

393 *in Exile, or the Tower:* After the accession of George I and the triumph of the Whigs, Bolingbroke, Ormonde, and (later) Bishop Atterbury were in exile, Oxford was in the Tower.

394 *within the Frown of Power:* "Upon the Queen's Death, the Dean returned to live in Dublin, at his Deanry-House: Numberless Libels were writ against him in England, as a Jacobite, he was insulted in the Streets, and at Nights was forced to be attended by his Servants armed." [Swift.]

395   Pursu'd by base envenom'd Pens,
      Far to the Land of Slaves and Fens;
      A servile Race in Folly nurs'd,
      Who truckle most, when treated worst.

      "By Innocence and Resolution,
400   He bore continual Persecution;
      While Numbers to Preferment rose;
      Whose Merits were, to be his Foes.
      When, *ev'n his own familiar Friends*
      Intent upon their private Ends;
405   Like Renegadoes now he feels,
      Against him lifting up their Heels.

      "The Dean did by his Pen defeat
      An infamous destructive Cheat.
      Taught Fools their Int'rest how to know;
410   And gave them Arms to ward the Blow.
      Envy hath own'd it was his doing,
      To save that helpless Land from Ruin,
      While they who at the Steerage stood,
      And reapt the Profit, sought his Blood.

415   "To save them from their evil Fate,
      In him was held a Crime of State.
      A wicked Monster on the Bench,

396 *Land of Slaves and Fens:* "The Land of Slaves and Fens, is Ireland." [Swift.]

408 *destructive Cheat:* "One Wood, a Hardware-man from England [who] had a Patent for coining Copper Half-pence in Ireland. . . ." [Swift.] For William Wood, see l. 168.

409 *Fools:* the Irish people.

413 *who at the Steerage stood:* who steered the ship of state. See note to l. 417.

417 *A wicked Monster:* "One Whitshed was then Chief Justice: He had some Years before prosecuted a Printer for a Pamphlet writ by the Dean, to perswade the People of Ireland to wear their own Manufactures [*A Proposal for the Universal Use of Irish Manufactures*, 1720]. Whitshed sent the

Whose Fury Blood could never quench;
As vile and profligate a Villain,
420 As modern Scroggs, or old Tressilian;
Who long all Justice had discarded,
Nor fear'd he GOD, nor Man regarded;
Vow'd on the Dean his Rage to vent,
And make him of his Zeal repent;
425 But Heav'n his Innocence defends,
The grateful People stand his Friends:
Not Strains of Law, nor Judges Frown,
Nor Topicks brought to please the Crown,
Nor Witness hir'd, nor Jury pick'd,
430 Prevail to bring him in convict.

"In Exile with a steady Heart,
He spent his Life's declining Part;
Where, Folly, Pride, and Faction sway,
Remote from St. John, Pope, and Gay.

435 "His Friendship there to few confin'd,
Were always of the midling Kind:
No Fools of Rank, a mungril Breed,
Who fain would pass for Lords indeed:

Jury down eleven Times, and kept them nine Hours, until they were forced
to bring in a special Verdict. He sat as Judge afterwards on the Tryal of the
Printer of the *Drapier's* Fourth Letter; but the Jury, against all he could say
or swear, threw out the Bill: All the Kingdom took the *Drapier's* Part,
except the Courtiers, or those who expected Places. . . ." [Swift.]

420 *Scroggs . . . Tressilian:* Sir William Scroggs, a time-serving judge in
the reign of Charles II, notorious for his brutality. Sir Robert Tresilian, a
Lord Chief Justice who behaved with great severity after the Peasants'
Revolt in the reign of Richard II, and was hanged in 1388.

427 *Strains of Law:* stretching the law.

430 *bring him in convict:* procure his conviction.

431 *In Exile:* in Ireland. Swift always thought of himself as an Englishman.

437 *No Fools of Rank:* "In Ireland the Dean was not acquainted with one
single Lord Spiritual or Temporal. He only conversed with private Gentlemen of the Clergy or Laity, and but a small number of either." [Swift.]

Where Titles give no Right or Power,
440 And Peerage is a wither'd Flower,
He would have held it a Disgrace,
If such a Wretch had known his Face.
On Rural Squires, that Kingdom's Bane,
He vented oft his Wrath in vain:
445 Biennial Squires, to Market brought;
Who sell their Souls and Votes for Naught;
The Nation stript go joyful back,
To rob the Church, their Tenants rack,
Go Snacks with Thieves and Rapparees,
450 And, keep the Peace, to pick up Fees:
In every Jobb to have a Share,
A Jayl or Barrack to repair;
And turn the Tax for publick Roads
Commodious to their own Abodes.

455   "Perhaps I may allow, the Dean
Had too much Satyr in his Vein;
And seem'd determin'd not to starve it,
Because no Age could more deserve it.
Yet, Malice never was his Aim;
460 He lash'd the Vice but spar'd the Name.

440 *Peerage is a wither'd Flower:* "The Peers of Ireland lost a great Part of their Jurisdiction by one single Act, and tamely submitted to this infamous Mark of Slavery without the least Resentment, or Remonstrance." [Swift.]

445 *Biennial Squires:* "The Parliament (as they call it) in Ireland meet but once in two Years; and, after giving five Times more than they can afford, return Home to reimburse themselves by all Country Jobs and Oppressions, of which some few only are here mentioned." [Swift.]

448 *rack:* extort unjustifiably high rents from.

449 *Go Snacks:* go shares.   *Rapparees:* highwaymen.

451 *Jobb:* a public service carried out with a view to lining the employer's pocket, a "racket" (as in the repairing of barracks for soldiers, l. 452).

460 *spar'd the Name:* This is hardly true. Swift mentioned several people by name in this poem, and many more in other satirical pieces. The claim is justified, however, by *Gulliver's Travels.*

No Individual could resent,
Where Thousands equally were meant.
His Satyr points at no Defect,
But what all Mortals may correct;
465 For he abhorr'd that senseless Tribe,
Who call it Humour when they jibe:
He spar'd a Hump or crooked Nose,
Whose Owners set not up for Beaux.
True genuine Dulness mov'd his Pity,
470 Unless it offer'd to be witty.
Those, who their Ignorance confess'd,
He ne'er offended with a Jest;
But laugh'd to hear an Idiot quote,
A Verse from Horace, learn'd by Rote.

475 "He knew an hundred pleasant Stories,
With all the Turns of Whigs and Tories:
Was chearful to his dying Day,
And Friends would let him have his Way.

"He gave the little Wealth he had,
480 To build a House for Fools and Mad:
And shew'd by one satyric Touch.
No Nation wanted it so much:
That Kingdom he hath left his Debtor,
I wish it soon may have a Better."

478 *Friends would let him have his Way:* i.e. they knew his eccentricities and accepted them.

480 *a House for Fools and Mad:* Swift left most of his money to found an asylum in Dublin for idiots and lunatics.

482 *That Kingdom:* "Meaning Ireland, where he now lives, and probably may dye." [Swift.]

Thomas Parnell

A NIGHT-PIECE ON DEATH

THE "Night Piece" is an interesting minor genre in eighteenth-century poetry. Meditations in churchyards, the contemplation of the night sky and reflections on death and on the uncertainty of life had become popular reading by the middle of the century. The prose *Meditations* (1745-7) of James Hervey had run through twenty-five editions by the 1790's, and must have equalled in popularity William Sherlock's *Practical Discourse concerning Death* (1689), a best seller of an earlier generation. Parnell's poem has neither the lapidary perfection nor the range of Gray's *Elegy*, and it tends, like *The Grave* of Robert Blair (1743), to dwell on the visible trappings of death; but commonplace thoughts and feelings are given a touch of solemn beauty by the ordered and controlled expression of Parnell's octosyllabic couplets. In 1722 Pope, who with Swift was a friend of Parnell, published a posthumous volume of his *Poems on Several Occasions*, from which the text is taken. Parnell was born in 1679 and died in 1718.

> By the blue Taper's trembling Light,
> No more I waste the wakeful Night,
> Intent with endless view to pore
> The Schoolmen and the Sages o'er:
> 5 Their Books from Wisdom widely stray,
> Or point at best the longest Way.
> I'll seek a readier Path, and go
> Where Wisdom's surely taught *below*.
>
> How deep yon Azure dies the Sky!
> 10 Where Orbs of Gold unnumber'd lye,
> While thro' their Ranks in silver pride
> The nether Crescent seems to glide.
> The slumb'ring Breeze forgets to breathe,
> The Lake is smooth and clear beneath,
> 15 Where once again the spangled Show
> Descends to meet our Eyes below.

4 *Schoolmen:* medieval theologians and philosophers.
8 *below:* i.e. underground, in the grave.

The Grounds which on the right aspire,
In dimness from the View retire:
The Left presents a Place of Graves,
20 Whose Wall the silent Water laves.
That Steeple guides thy doubtful sight
Among the livid gleams of Night.
There pass with melancholy State,
By all the solemn Heaps of Fate,
25 And think, as softly-sad you tread
Above the venerable Dead,
Time was, like Thee they Life possest,
And Time shall be, that thou shalt Rest.

Those Graves, with bending Osier bound,
30 That nameless heave the crumbled Ground,
Quick to the glancing Thought disclose
Where *Toil* and *Poverty* repose.

The flat smooth Stones that bear a Name,
The Chissels slender help to Fame,
35 (Which e'er our Sett of Friends decay
Their frequent Steps may wear away)
A *middle Race* of Mortals own,
Men, half ambitious, all unknown.

The Marble Tombs that rise on high,
40 Whose Dead in vaulted Arches lye,
Whose Pillars swell with sculptur'd Stones,
Arms, Angels, Epitaphs and Bones,
These (all the poor Remains of State)
Adorn the *Rich*, or praise the *Great*;
45 Who while on Earth in Fame they live,
Are sensless of the Fame they give.

Ha! while I gaze, pale Cynthia fades,
The bursting Earth unveils the Shades!

22 *livid:* literally, "of a bluish leaden colour".
48 *Shades:* ghosts.

All slow, and wan, and wrap'd with Shrouds,
50   They rise in visionary Crouds,
And all with sober Accent cry,
Think, Mortal, what it is to dye.

Now from yon black and fun'ral Yew,
That bathes the Charnel House with Dew,
55   Methinks I hear a *Voice* begin;
(Ye Ravens, cease your croaking Din,
Ye tolling Clocks, no Time resound
O'er the long Lake and midnight Ground)
It sends a Peal of hollow Groans
60   Thus speaking from among the Bones:

When Men my Scythe and Darts supply
How great a *King* of *Fears* am I!
They view me like the last of Things:
They make , and then they dread, my Stings.
65   Fools! if you less provok'd your Fears
No more my Spectre-Form appears.
Death's but a Path that must be trod
If Man wou'd ever pass to God:
A Port of Calms, a State of Ease
70   From the rough Rage of swelling Seas.

Why then thy flowing sable Stoles,
Deep pendent Cypress, mourning Poles,
Loose Scarfs to fall athwart thy Weeds,
Long Palls, drawn Herses, cover'd Steeds,

61 *supply:* i.e. furnish from the imagination.

71 *Stoles:* long (mourning) robes. Cf. Milton, "Il Penseroso", l. 35: "And sable Stole of Cypress Lawn."

72 *Cypress:* a light material like crape, which, when black, was much used for mourning.   *Poles:* black staffs carried in a funeral procession.

73 *Scarfs:* scarves of black silk or crape worn at funerals.

74 *cover'd Steeds:* horses drawing the hearse, covered with heavy black cloth.

75   And Plumes of black, that as they tread,
      Nod o'er the 'Scutcheons of the Dead?

      Nor can the parted Body know,
      Nor wants the Soul, these Forms of Woe:
      As Men who long in Prison dwell,
80   With Lamps that glimmer round the Cell,
      When e'er their suffering Years are run,
      Spring forth to greet the glitt'ring Sun:
      Such Joy, tho' far transcending Sense,
      Have pious Souls at parting hence.
85   On Earth, and in the Body plac't,
      A few, and evil Years, they wast:
      But when their Chains are cast aside,
      See the glad Scene unfolding wide,
      Clap the glad Wing and tow'r away,
90   And mingle with the Blaze of Day.

76 *'Scutcheons:* The escutcheon was an armorial tablet exhibiting the armorial bearings of a deceased person. In the above lines Parnell has run through some of the main features of eighteenth-century funeral pomp.

89 *tow'r:* soar.

Ambrose Philips

A WINTER-PIECE
TO THE EARL OF DORSET

Copenhagen, March 9, 1709

IN January, 1709, Philips went to Denmark as secretary to the English ambassador, and from there he sent this "winter-piece" to Addison, who duly had it published in *The Tatler*, May 7, 1709. "Such images as these," Steele wrote, "give us a new pleasure in our sight." Philips had indeed captured very well the unfamiliar and artificial beauty of a frost-bound landscape. In his descriptions of Nature the eighteenth-century poet is often at his best when Nature comes nearest to being already in effect a work of art.

From Frozen Climes, and Endless Tracks of Snow,
From Streams that Northern Winds forbid to flow;
What Present shall the Muse to Dorset bring;
Or how, so near the Pole, attempt to sing?
5 The hoary Winter here conceals from Sight
All pleasing Objects that to Verse invite.
The Hills and Dales, and the Delightful Woods,
The Flowry Plains, and Silver Streaming Floods,
By Snow disguised, in bright Confusion lye,
10 And with one dazling Waste fatigue the Eye.
    No gentle breathing Breeze prepares the Spring,
No Birds within the Desert Region sing.
The Ships unmov'd the boist'rous Winds defy,
While rattling Chariots o'er the Ocean fly.
15 The vast Leviathan wants Room to play,
And spout his Waters in the Face of Day.
The starving Wolves along the main Sea prowl,
And to the Moon in Icy Valleys howl.
For many a shining League the level Main
20 Here spreads it self into a Glassy Plain:
There solid Billows of enormous Size,
Alpes of green Ice, in wild Disorder rise.
    And yet but lately have I seen, e'en here,
The Winter in a lovely Dress appear.
25 E'er yet the Clouds let fall the treasur'd Snow,
Or Winds begun thro' hazy Skies to blow.
At Ev'ning a keen Eastern Breeze arose;
And the descending Rain unsullied froze.
Soon as the silent Shades of Night withdrew,
30 The ruddy Morning disclos'd at once to View
The Face of Nature in a rich Disguise,
And brighten'd ev'ry Object to my Eyes.
For ev'ry Shrub, and ev'ry Blade of Grass,
And ev'ry pointed Thorn, seem'd wrought in Glass.
35 In Pearls and Rubies rich the Hawthorns show,
While thro' the Ice the Crimson Berries glow.

---

3 *Dorset:* the 7th Earl of Dorset, who was at this time Philips's patron.

The thick-sprung Reeds the watry Marches yield,
Seem polish'd Lances in a hostile Field.
The Stag in limpid Currents with Surprize
40   Sees Chrystal Branches on his Forehead rise.
The spreading Oak, the Beech, and tow'ring Pine,
Glaz'd over, in the freezing Æther shine.
The frighted Birds the rattling Branches shun,
That wave and glitter in the distant Sun.
45   When if a sudden Gust of Wind arise,
The Brittle Forrest into Atoms flies:
The crackling Wood beneath the Tempest bends,
And in a spangled Show'r the Prospect ends.
Or if a Southern Gale the Region warm,
50   And by Degrees unbind the Wintry Charm;
The Traveller a miry Country sees,
And Journeys sad beneath the dropping Trees.

TO MISS CHARLOTTE PULTENEY
IN HER MOTHER'S ARMS

PHILIPS, who remained a bachelor all his life, acted as a sort of voluntary uncle to several little girls, the daughters of Lord Carteret and Sir William Pulteney, and wrote various poems of a "Christopher Robin" kind for them, which earned him a good deal of ridicule and the nick-name of Namby-Pamby. One would hardly expect Swift or Pope to be in sympathy with his rather artificial simplicity, but even a more indulgent reader may recoil from a poem which begins "Dimply damsel, sweetly smiling . . ." Philips was at his most mawkish in some lines addressed to one of Lord Carteret's daughters, "Bloom of beauty, early flow'r"; but in the following verses to Charlotte Pulteney, he is sentimental without being childish. For a parody of his "infantine" style, see p. 189.

Timely blossom, infant fair,
Fondling of a happy pair,
Every morn, and every night,
Their solicitous delight,
5   Sleeping, waking, still at ease,
Pleasing, without skill to please,

Little gossip, blithe and hale,
Tatling many a broken tale,
Singing many a tuneless song,
10 Lavish of a heedless tongue,
Simple maiden, void of art,
Babbling out the very heart,
Yet abandon'd to thy will,
Yet imagining no ill,
15 Yet too innocent to blush,
Like the linlet in the bush,
To the Mother-linnet's note
Moduling her slender throat,
Chirping forth thy petty joys,
20 Wanton in the change of toys,
Like the linnet green, in May,
Flitting to each bloomy spray,
Wearied then, and glad of rest,
Like the linlet in the nest.
25 This thy present happy lot,
This, in time, will be forgot:
Other pleasures, other cares,
Ever-busy time prepares;
And thou shalt in thy daughter see,
30 This picture, once, resembled thee.

16 *linlet:* This word (repeated at l. 24) appears to be used by the poet to refer to the fledgling linnet, as distinct from the mother bird.

Alexander Pope

THE RAPE OF THE LOCK
An Heroi-Comical Poem
In Five Cantos

Nolueram, Belinda, tuos violare capillos,
Sed juvat hoc precibus me tribuisse tuis.★

"WHAT mighty Contests rise from trivial Things!" Some time in the year 1711 a playful young peer, Lord Petre, snipped off a lock of Miss Arabella Fermor's hair, and so provoked a quarrel between their two families. A common friend, John Caryll, suggested to Pope that he might write a poem ridiculing the whole silly business, and so restore a sense of proportion to the estranged families and, as Pope put it, "laugh them together again". Pope set to work, and "in less than a fortnight's time" produced the original version of *The Rape of the Lock*, which, as a poem in two cantos, was published in Lintot's *Miscellany* of 1712. (Shortly before it appeared Lord Petre had married a Lancashire heiress.) Two years later (Lord Petre having meanwhile died of smallpox) *The Rape of the Lock* appeared in its final form in five cantos, the chief addition being that of the sylphs. It quickly ran through three editions in 1714, and in the long run it has proved to be Pope's most popular poem.

It is, as he says, "an heroi-comical" or mock-heroic poem, and as such it belongs to a *genre* that became very popular in the seventeenth and eighteenth centuries, when the heroic poem was also at the height of its popularity. In ancient literature the kind is represented by Homer's lost *Margites* and by his *Batrachomuomachia* (translated by Parnell as "The Battle of the Frogs and the Mice"); and in modern times by such poems as Tassoni's *Secchia Rapita* (in its English version "The Rape of the Bucket"), Boileau's *Le Lutrin*, and *The Dispensary* of Sir Samuel Garth. The mock-heroic is to be distinguished from travesty or burlesque: in the latter, as Boileau said, Dido is made to talk like a fishwife; in the former, unheroic characters talk like Dido and Æneas, and mock importance is given to trivial activities which ironically reflect the serious concerns of epic poetry. While the reader of *The Rape of the Lock* is aware of the mock-heroic element throughout, he is also very conscious of the beauty of the artificial world in which Pope has involved his characters, and of the comic imagination that has created the delicate sylphs. Pope's reputation as a poet fell sharply in the

★ Martial, XII, lxxxiv. 1-2. (Pope has substituted "Belinda" for Martial's "Polytime".)

nineteenth century, and among the Romantic poets only Byron spoke up for him. "Because he is always intelligible," Byron complained, "it is taken for granted that he is the 'Poet of Reason', as if that was a reason for his being no poet." Yet even in the nineteenth century those who thought of Pope as a poet of reason (and therefore a poet of a lower order) were forced to make some kind of exception, however reluctantly, of *The Rape of the Lock*.

TO MRS.* ARABELLA FERMOR

Madam,

It will be in vain to deny that I have some Regard for this Piece, since I Dedicate it to You. Yet You may bear me Witness, it was intended only to divert a few young Ladies, who have good Sense and good Humour enough, to laugh not only at their Sex's little unguarded Follies, but at their own. But as it was communicated with the Air of a Secret, it soon found its Way into the World. An imperfect Copy having been offer'd to a Bookseller, You had the Good-Nature for my Sake to consent to the Publication of one more correct: This I was forc'd to before I had executed half my Design, for the Machinery was entirely wanting to compleat it.

The Machinery, Madam, is a Term invented by the Criticks, to signify that Part which the Deities, Angels, or Dæmons, are made to act in a Poem: For the ancient Poets are in one respect like many modern Ladies; Let an Action be never so trivial in it self, they always make it appear of the utmost Importance. These Machines I determin'd to raise on a very new and odd Foundation, the Rosicrucian† Doctrine of Spirits.

I know how disagreeable it is to make use of hard Words before a Lady; but 'tis so much the Concern of a Poet to have his Works understood, and particularly by your Sex, that You must give me leave to explain two or three difficult Terms.

The Rosicrucians are a People I must bring You acquainted with. The best Account I know of them is in a French Book call'd *Le*

(*) *Mrs:* i.e. Miss. At this period "Mrs." was used for addressing married and unmarried ladies alike.

(†) *the Rosicrucian Doctrine:* The Rosicrucians were an order or society whose members claimed to have power over the elements and elemental spirits. *Le Comte de Gabalis* which Pope goes on to mention was by the Abbé de Montfaucon Villars, and had been translated into English in 1680.

Comte de Gabalis, which both in its Title and Size is so like a Novel, that many of the Fair Sex have read it for one by Mistake. According to these Gentlemen, the four Elements are inhabited by Spirits, which they call *Sylphs, Gnomes, Nymphs,* and *Salamanders.* The Gnomes, or Dæmons of Earth, delight in Mischief; but the Sylphs, whose Habitation is in the Air, are the best-condition'd Creatures imaginable. For they say, any Mortals may enjoy the most intimate Familiarities with these gentle Spirits, upon a Condition very easie to all true Adepts, an inviolate Preservation of Chastity.

As to the following Canto's, all the Passages of them are as Fabulous, as the Vision at the Beginning, or the Transformation at the End; (except the Loss of your Hair, which I always mention with Reverence.) The Human Persons are as Fictitious as the Airy ones; and the Character of Belinda, as it is now manag'd, resembles You in nothing but in Beauty.

If this Poem had as many Graces as there are in Your Person, or in Your Mind, yet I could never hope it should pass thro' the World half so Uncensured as You have done. But let its Fortune be what it will, mine is happy enough, to have given me this Occasion of assuring You that I am, with the truest Esteem,

Madam,

Your Most Obedient
Humble Servant,

A. POPE.

CANTO I

What dire Offence from am'rous Causes springs,
What mighty Contests rise from trivial Things,
I sing—This Verse to Caryll, Muse! is due;
This ev'n Belinda may vouchsafe to view:
5   Slight is the Subject, but not so the Praise,
If She inspire, and He approve my Lays,
    Say what strange Motive, Goddess! cou'd compel
A well-bred *Lord* t'assault a gentle *Belle?*

1-12 Pope opens his poem with two features of classical epic poetry: a "proposition" or statement of the theme (1-3), and an invocation to some god or goddess—here Belinda herself, the inspirer of his lays.

Oh say what stranger Cause, yet unexplor'd,
10 Cou'd make a gentle *Belle* reject a *Lord?*
In Tasks so bold, can Little Men engage,
And in soft Bosoms dwells such mighty Rage?
    Sol thro' white Curtains shot a tim'rous Ray,
And op'd those Eyes that must eclipse the Day;
15 Now Lapdogs give themselves the rowzing Shake,
And sleepless Lovers, just at Twelve, awake;
Thrice rung the Bell, the Slipper knock'd the Ground,
And the press'd Watch return'd a silver Sound.
Belinda still her downy Pillow prest,
20 Her Guardian Sylph prolong'd the balmy Rest.
'Twas he had summon'd to her silent Bed
The Morning-Dream that hover'd o'er her Head.
A Youth more glitt'ring than a *Birth-night Beau*,
(That ev'n in Slumber caus'd her Cheek to glow)
25 Seem'd to her Ear his winning Lips to lay,
And thus in Whispers said, or seem'd to say.
    Fairest of Mortals, thou distinguish'd Care
Of thousand bright Inhabitants of Air!
If e'er one Vision touch'd thy infant Thought,
30 Of all the Nurse and all the Priest have taught,
Of airy Elves by Moonlight Shadows seen,
The silver Token, and the circled Green,

11 *Little Men:* Lord Petre was a small-sized man, a circumstance that fitted him well for the mock-heroic.

17 *Thrice rung the Bell:* Such triple repetition is often found in epic poetry. Cf. also iii. 137-8.   The slipper "knock'd the Ground" because Belinda, failing to get any reply to her ringing of a hand-bell, tries what knocking on the floor with her slipper will do.

18 *the press'd Watch:* "Repeater" watches, which sounded the hour and the quarters, were a fairly recent and fashionable innovation.

23 *Birth-night Beau:* He is going to a royal birthday party at Court, and is therefore dressed with especial splendour.

32 *The silver Token:* the silver coin said to be left by fairies to be picked up by some industrious maid.   *the circled Green:* the grass marked by a fairy ring.

Or Virgins visited by Angel-Pow'rs,
With Golden Crowns and Wreaths of heavn'ly Flow'rs,
35 Hear and believe! thy own Importance know,
Nor bound thy narrow Views to Things below.
Some secret Truths from Learned Pride conceal'd,
To Maids alone and Children are reveal'd:
What tho' no Credit doubting Wits may give?
40 The Fair and Innocent shall still believe.
Know then, unnumber'd Spirits round thee fly,
The light Militia of the lower Sky;
These, tho' unseen, are ever on the Wing,
Hang o'er the Box, and hover round the Ring.
45 Think what an Equipage thou hast in Air,
And view with scorn Two Pages and a Chair.
As now your own, our Beings were of old,
And once inclos'd in Woman's beauteous Mold;
Thence, by a soft Transition, we repair
50 From earthly Vehicles to these of Air,
Think not, when Woman's transient Breath is fled,
That all her Vanities at once are dead:
Succeeding Vanities she still regards,
And tho' she plays no more, o'erlooks the Cards.
55 Her Joy in gilded Chariots, when alive,
And Love of Ombre, after Death survive.
For when the Fair in all their Pride expire,
To their first Elements their Souls retire:

33 *Virgins visited:* as the Virgin Mary and some virgin saints.

37-8 See *Matthew*, xi, 25.

44 *the Box:* i.e. in the theatre.   *the Ring:* the fashionable drive in Hyde Park.

46 *Chair:* a sedan chair.

50 *earthly Vehicles:* i.e. bodies, the material forms in which the soul is embodied.

54 *o'erlooks:* stands behind the players watching the game.

55-6 *Her Joy . . . survive:* an imitation of Virgil, *Aeneid,* vi, 653-5, and, more immediately, of Dryden's translation: "The love of horses which they had, alive,/And care of chariots, after death survive."

56 *Ombre:* For ombre, a card game, see iii, 27.

58 *first:* preponderating.

The Sprights of fiery Termagants in Flame
60 Mount up, and take a Salamander's Name.
Soft yielding Minds to Water glide away,
And sip with Nymphs, their Elemental Tea.
The graver Prude sinks downward to a Gnome,
In search of Mischief still on Earth to roam.
65 The light Coquettes in Sylphs aloft repair,
And sport and flutter in the Fields of Air.
    Know farther yet; Whoever fair and chaste
Rejects Mankind, is by some Sylph embrac'd:
For Spirits, freed from mortal Laws, with ease
70 Assume what Sexes and what Shapes they please.
What guards the Purity of melting Maids,
In Courtly Balls, and Midnight Masquerades,
Safe from the treach'rous Friend, the daring Spark,
The Glance by Day, the Whisper in the Dark;
75 When kind Occasion prompts their warm Desires,
When Musick softens, and when Dancing fires?
'Tis but their Sylph, the wise Celestials know,
Tho' *Honour* is the Word with Men below.
    Some Nymphs there are, too conscious of their Face,
80 For Life predestin'd to the Gnomes' Embrace.
These swell their Prospects and exalt their Pride,
When Offers are disdain'd, and Love deny'd.
Then gay Ideas crowd the vacant Brain;
While Peers and Dukes, and all their sweeping Train,
85 And Garters, Stars and Coronets appear,
And in soft Sounds, *Your Grace* salutes their Ear.

59 *Termagants:* quarrelsome women.

62 *Tea:* at this period regularly pronounced "tay".

66 *Fields of Air:* Dryden's translation of a phrase in *Aeneid*, i, 196.

72 *Masquerades:* assemblies in fancy dress, usually accompanied with dancing. Since both men and women wore masks, behaviour was often a good deal freer than moralists could approve.

81 *Prospects:* expectations.

85 *Garters, Stars:* Garters are worn by Knights of the Garter: stars, by Knights of the Garter, the Thistle, and the Bath—the chief orders in Pope's day.

'Tis these that early taint the Female Soul,
Instruct the Eyes of young Coquettes to roll,
Teach Infant-Cheeks a bidden Blush to know,
90 And little Hearts to flutter at a Beau.
     Oft when the World imagine Women stray,
The Sylphs thro' mystick Mazes guide their Way,
Thro' all the giddy Circle they pursue,
And old Impertinence expel by new.
95 What tender Maid but must a Victim fall
To one Man's Treat, but for another's Ball?
When Floria speaks, what Virgin could withstand,
If gentle Damon did not squeeze her Hand?
With varying Vanities, from ev'ry Part,
100 They shift the moving Toyshop of their Heart;
Where Wigs with Wigs, with Sword-knots Sword-knots
          strive,
Beaus banish Beaus, and Coaches Coaches drive.
This erring Mortals Levity may call,
Oh blind to Truth! the Sylphs contrive it all.
105   Of these am I, who thy Protection claim,
A watchful Sprite, and *Ariel* is my Name.
Late, as I rang'd the Crystal Wilds of Air,
In the clear Mirror of thy ruling Star
I saw, alas! some dread Event impend,
110 Ere to the Main this Morning Sun descend.
But Heav'n reveals not what, or how, or where:
Warn'd by the Sylph, oh Pious Maid beware!

89 *a bidden Blush:* i.e. the red of rouge.

94 *Impertinence:* triviality.

96 *Treat:* an entertainment of food and drink.

99-102 Pope took a hint for this passage from *The Guardian,* July 13, 1713, where Addison had referred to the heart of a fashionable young lady as a "toyshop", and had described the sort of things that were to be found in it.

101 *Sword-knots:* ribbons tied to the hilts of swords.

105 *who thy Protection claim:* i.e. who claim to be allowed to protect you.

109 *dread Event:* Omens, portents, etc. are a feature of epic poetry.

This to disclose is all thy Guardian can.
Beware of all, but most beware of Man!
115   He said; when *Shock*, who thought she slept too long,
Leapt up, and wak'd his Mistress with his Tongue.
'Twas then Belinda! if Report say true,
Thy Eyes first open'd on a *Billet-doux*;
Wounds, *Charms*, and *Ardors*, were no sooner read,
120 But all the Vision vanish'd from thy Head.
    And now, unveil'd, the Toilet stands display'd,
Each Silver Vase in mystic Order laid.
First, rob'd in White, the Nymph intent adores
With Head uncover'd, the Cosmetic Pow'rs.
125 A heav'nly Image in the Glass appears,
To that she bends, to that her Eyes she rears;
Th' inferior Priestess, at her Altar's side,
Trembling, begins the sacred Rites of Pride.
Unnumber'd Treasures ope at once, and here
130 The various Off'rings of the World appear;
From each she nicely culls with curious Toil,
And decks the Goddess with the glitt'ring Spoil.
This Casket India's glowing Gems unlocks,
And all Arabia breathes from yonder Box.
135 The Tortoise here and Elephant unite,
Transform'd to *Combs*, the speckled and the white.
Here Files of Pins extend their shining Rows,
Puffs, Powders, Patches, Bibles, Billet-doux.
Now awful Beauty puts on all its Arms;
140 The Fair each moment rises in her Charms,
Repairs her Smiles, awakens ev'ry Grace,
And calls forth all the Wonders of her Face;

115 *Shock:* The shock was a rough-haired lapdog popular with ladies.

119 *Wounds . . . Ardors:* the fashionable terminology of eighteenth-century love-letters.

127 *Th' inferior Priestess:* Belinda's maid.

138 *Patches:* small pieces of black silk worn on the face by fashionable ladies. Cf. *Trivia*, p. 142, l. 120.

139 ff. The next few lines are a parody of the arming of a hero in epic poetry.

Sees by Degrees a purer Blush arise,
And keener Lightnings quicken in her Eyes.
145   The busy Sylphs surround their darling Care;
These set the Head, and those divide the Hair,
Some fold the Sleeve, whilst others plait the Gown;
And Betty's prais'd for Labours not her own.

CANTO II

Not with more Glories, in th' Etherial Plain,
The Sun first rises o'er the purpled Main,
Than issuing forth, the Rival of his Beams
Lanch'd on the Bosom of the Silver Thames.
5   Fair Nymphs, and well-drest Youths around her shone,
But ev'ry Eye was fix'd on her alone.
On her white Breast a sparkling Cross she wore,
Which Jews might kiss, and Infidels adore.
Her lively Looks a sprightly Mind disclose,
10   Quick as her Eyes, and as unfix'd as those:
Favours to none, to all she Smiles extends,
Oft she rejects, but never once offends.
Bright as the Sun, her Eyes the Gazers strike,
And, like the Sun, they shine on all alike.
15   Yet graceful Ease, and Sweetness void of Pride,
Might hide her Faults, if Belles had Faults to hide:
If to her share some Female Errors fall,
Look on her Face, and you'll forget 'em all.
   This Nymph, to the Destruction of Mankind,
20   Nourish'd two Locks, which graceful hung behind

143 *a purer Blush:* The blush is obtained by Belinda's rouge. The word "purer" may be merely ironical, but "pure" was also used colloquially in Pope's day to mean "fine", "splendid".

144 *keener Lightnings:* Professor Tillotson's note in the "Twickenham" edition suggest that Belinda has been using belladonna to enlarge the pupils of the eye, or that she has darkened the surrounding skin.

146 *the Head:* In Queen Anne's day fashionable ladies wore their hair in a high "tower" or "head" supported by pasteboard and muslin.

20 *Nourish'd:* in the sense of "grew", but perhaps also of "cherished".

In equal Curls, and well conspir'd to deck
With shining Ringlets the smooth Iv'ry Neck.
Love in these Labyrinths his Slaves detains,
And mighty Hearts are held in slender Chains.
25 With hairy Sprindges we the Birds betray,
Slight Lines of Hair surprize the Finny Prey,
Fair Tresses Man's Imperial Race insnare,
And Beauty draws us with a single Hair.
    Th' Adventrous Baron the bright Locks admir'd,
30 He saw, he wish'd, and to the Prize aspir'd:
Resolv'd to win, he meditates the way,
By Force to ravish, or by Fraud betray;
For when Success a Lover's Toil attends,
Few ask, if Fraud or Force attain'd his Ends.
35   For this, ere Phœbus rose, he had implor'd
Propitious Heav'n, and ev'ry Pow'r ador'd,
But chiefly *Love*—to *Love* an Altar built,
Of twelve vast French Romances, neatly gilt.
There lay three Garters, half a Pair of Gloves;
40 And all the Trophies of his former Loves.
With tender *Billet-doux* he lights the Pyre,
And breathes three am'rous Sighs to raise the Fire.
Then prostrate falls, and begs with ardent Eyes
Soon to obtain, and long possess the Prize:
45 The Pow'rs gave Ear, and granted half his Pray'r,
The rest, the Winds dispers'd in empty Air.
    But now secure the painted Vessel glides,
The Sun-beams trembling on the floating Tydes,
While melting Musick steals upon the Sky,
50 And soften'd Sounds along the Waters die.

25 *Sprindges:* snares.

37 *an Altar built:* The hero in epic poetry frequently sacrifices to some god before an important action.

38 *vast French Romances:* Seventeenth-century prose romances (by La Calprenède, Mlle. de Scudéry, etc.) were still upper-class reading. They were usually of great length, and often published in folio.

46 *the Winds dispers'd . . . Air:* an imitation of *Aeneid*, xi, 795; but the notion is common in classical poetry.

Smooth flow the Waves, the Zephyrs gently play,
Belinda smil'd, and all the World was gay.
All but the Sylph—With careful Thoughts opprest,
Th' impending Woe sate heavy on his Breast.
55 He summons strait his Denizens of Air;
The lucid Squadrons round the Sails repair:
Soft o'er the Shrouds Aerial Whispers breathe,
That seem'd but Zephyrs to the Train beneath.
Some to the Sun their Insect-Wings unfold,
60 Waft on the Breeze, or sink in Clouds of Gold.
Transparent Forms, too fine for mortal Sight,
Their fluid Bodies half dissolv'd in Light.
Loose to the Wind their airy Garments flew,
Thin glitt'ring Textures of the filmy Dew;
65 Dipt in the richest Tincture of the Skies,
Where Light disports in ever-mingling Dies,
While ev'ry Beam new transient Colours flings,
Colours that change whene'er they wave their Wings.
Amid the Circle, on the gilded Mast,
70 Superior by the Head, was Ariel plac'd;
His Purple Pinions opening to the Sun,
He rais'd his Azure Wand, and thus begun.
    Ye Sylphs and Sylphids, to your Chief give Ear,
Fays, Fairies, Genii, Elves, and Dæmons hear!
75 Ye know the Spheres and various Tasks assign'd,
By Laws Eternal, to th' Aerial Kind.
Some in the Fields of purest Æther play,
And bask and whiten in the Blaze of Day.
Some guide the Course of wandring Orbs on high,
80 Or roll the Planets thro' the boundless Sky.
Some less refin'd, beneath the Moon's pale Light
Pursue the Stars that shoot athwart the Night,

53 *careful:* full of care, anxious.

64 *the filmy Dew:* It used to be thought that the gossamer spun by spiders in the autumn was produced by sunburnt dew.

70 *Superior by the Head:* a head taller, as epic heroes almost invariably are.

73 *Sylphids:* young sylphs.

Or suck the Mists in grosser Air below,
Or dip their Pinions in the painted Bow,
85 Or brew fierce Tempests on the wintry Main,
Or o'er the Glebe, distill the kindly Rain.
Others on Earth o'er human Race preside,
Watch all their Ways, and all their Actions guide:
Of these the Chief the Care of Nations own,
90 And guard with Arms Divine the British Throne.
    Our humbler Province is to tend the Fair,
Not a less pleasing, tho' less glorious Care.
To save the Powder from too rude a Gale,
Nor let th' imprison'd Essences exhale,
95 To draw fresh Colours from the vernal Flow'rs,
To steal from Rainbows ere they drop in Show'rs
A brighter Wash; to curl their waving Hairs,
Assist their Blushes, and inspire their Airs;
Nay oft, in Dreams, Invention we bestow,
100 To change a Flounce, or add a Furbelow.
    This Day, black Omens threat the brightest Fair
That e'er deserv'd a watchful Spirit's Care;
Some dire Disaster, or by Force, or Slight,
But what, or where, the Fates have wrapt in Night.
105 Whether the Nymph shall break Diana's Law,
Or some frail China Jar receive a Flaw,
Or stain her Honour, or her new Brocade,
Forget her Pray'rs, or miss a Masquerade,
Or lose her Heart, or Necklace, at a Ball;
110 Or whether Heav'n has doom'd that *Shock* must fall.
Haste then ye Spirits! to your Charge repair;
The flutt'ring Fan be Zephyretta's Care;
The Drops to thee, Brillante, we consign;
And, Momentilla, let the Watch be thine;

91 *tend:* attend, wait upon.
100 *Furbelow:* a piece of stuff pleated and puckered on a gown or petticoat.
103 *Slight:* i.e. sleight.
105 *break Diana's Law:* lose her virginity.
113 *Drops:* diamonds hanging in the ear. Cf. l. 140, and iii, 137.

115   Do thou, Crispissa, tend her fav'rite Lock;
        Ariel himself shall be the Guard of *Shock*.
            To Fifty chosen Sylphs, of special Note,
        We trust th' important Charge, the Petticoat:
        Oft have we known that sev'nfold Fence to fail,
120   Tho' stiff with Hoops, and arm'd with Ribs of Whale.
        Form a strong Line about the Silver Bound,
        And guard the wide Circumference around.
            Whatever Spirit, careless of his Charge,
        His Post neglects, or leaves the Fair at large,
125   Shall feel sharp Vengeance soon o'ertake his Sins,
        Be stopt in Vials, or transfixt with Pins;
        Or plung'd in Lakes of bitter Washes lie,
        Or wedg'd whole Ages in a Bodkin's Eye:
        Gums and Pomatums shall his Flight restrain,
130   While clog'd he beats his silken Wings in vain;
        Or Alom-Stypticks with contracting Power
        Shrink his thin Essence like a rivell'd Flower.
        Or as Ixion fix'd, the Wretch shall feel
        The giddy Motion of the whirling Mill,
135   In Fumes of burning Chocolate shall glow,
        And tremble at the Sea that froaths below!
            He spoke; the Spirits from the Sails descend;
        Some, Orb in Orb, around the Nymph extend,
        Some thrid the mazy Ringlets of her Hair,
140   Some hang upon the Pendants of her Ear;
        With beating Hearts the dire Event they wait,
        Anxious, and trembling for the Birth of Fate.

115 *Crispissa:* The names of the various sylphs suit the occupations assigned to them: to "crisp" is to curl or crimp the hair.

119 *sev'nfold:* a Homeric epithet, not to be taken literally.

120 *Hoops:* The hooped petticoat, varying in width, remained in fashion for most of the century.   **126** *Vials:* here probably scent-bottles.

131 *Alom-Stypticks:* used to remove spots or pimples.

132 *rivell'd:* wrinkled.

133 *Ixion:* He tried to seduce Juno, and was condemned by Jove to be tied to a wheel in Hell which whirled round continually.

134 *Mill:* for grinding chocolate.

CANTO III

Close by those Meads for ever crown'd with Flow'rs,
Where Thames with Pride surveys his rising Tow'rs,
There stands a Structure of Majestick Frame,
Which from the neighb'ring Hampton takes its Name.
5 Here Britain's Statesmen oft the Fall foredoom
Of Foreign Tyrants, and of Nymphs at home;
Here Thou, Great Anna! whom three Realms obey,
Dost sometimes Counsel take—and sometimes Tea.
   Hither the Heroes and the Nymphs resort,
10 To taste awhile the Pleasures of a Court;
In various Talk th' instructive hours they past,
Who gave the Ball, or paid the Visit last:
One speaks the Glory of the British Queen,
And one describes a charming Indian Screen;
15 A third interprets Motions, Looks, and Eyes;
At ev'ry Word a Reputation dies.
Snuff, or the Fan, supply each Pause of Chat,
With singing, laughing, ogling, and all that.
   Mean while declining from the Noon of Day,
20 The Sun obliquely shoots his burning Ray;
The hungry Judges soon the Sentence sign,
And Wretches hang that Jury-men may Dine;
The Merchant from th' Exchange returns in Peace,
And the long Labours of the *Toilette* cease—
25 Belinda now, whom Thirst of Fame invites,
Burns to encounter two adventrous Knights,
At Ombre singly to decide their Doom;
And swells her Breast with Conquests yet to come.

3 *a Structure:* Hampton Court, built by Cardinal Wolsey in the reign of Henry VIII, and enlarged by William III, who often stayed there. Queen Anne preferred Windsor.

7 *three Realms:* possibly England, Ireland and Scotland; but Queen Anne was styled Queen of Great Britain, France and Ireland.

27 *Ombre:* a card game for three players. For an account of the game in the context of this poem, see *The Rape of the Lock and Other Poems*, ed. Geoffrey Tillotson ("Twickenham" edition). The whole episode of the card game parodies the battles of epic poetry.

Strait the three Bands prepare in Arms to join,
30   Each Band the number of the Sacred Nine.
Soon as she spreads her Hand, th' Aerial Guard
Descend, and sit on each important Card:
First Ariel perch'd upon a Matadore,
Then each, according to the Rank they bore;
35   For Sylphs, yet mindful of their ancient Race,
Are, as when Women, wondrous fond of Place.
  Behold, four *Kings* in Majesty rever'd,
With hoary Whiskers and a forky Beard;
And four fair *Queens* whose hands sustain a Flow'r,
40   Th' expressive Emblem of their softer Pow'r;
Four *Knaves* in Garbs succinct, a trusty Band,
Caps on their heads, and Halberds in their hand;
And Particolour'd Troops, a shining Train,
Draw forth to Combat on the Velvet Plain.
45   The skilful Nymph reviews her Force with Care;
Let Spades be Trumps! she said, and Trumps they were.
  Now move to War her Sable Matadores,
In Show like Leaders of the swarthy Moors.
Spadillio first, unconquerable Lord!
50   Led off two captive Trumps, and swept the Board.
As many more Manillio forc'd to yield,
And march'd a Victor from the verdant Field.
Him *Basto* follow'd, but his Fate more hard
Gain'd but one Trump and one Plebeian Card.
55   With his broad Sabre next, a Chief in Years,
The hoary Majesty of Spades appears;

  30 *Nine:* the number of cards dealt to each ombre player.
  33 *Matadore:* The matadores were the Aces of Spades and Clubs, and one other card (depending upon which suit was trumps).
    36 *Place:* rank.   **41** *succinct:* close-fitting.
    44 *Velvet Plain:* i.e. the velvet-covered card-table.
  46 *Let Spades be Trumps!:* Belinda has taken on the other two players, and so become "ombre" (Spanish *hombre* = man). She is now entitled to name trumps.   **49** *Spadillio:* Ace of Spades.
  51 *Manillio:* the Two of Spades, next in value to the Ace.
  53 *Basto:* Ace of Clubs.

Puts forth one manly Leg, to sight reveal'd;
The rest his many-colour'd Robe conceal'd.
The Rebel-*Knave*, who dares his Prince engage,
60 Proves the just Victim of his Royal Rage.
Ev'n mighty Pam that Kings and Queens o'erthrew,
And mow'd down Armies in the Fights of Lu,
Sad Chance of War! now, destitute of Aid,
Falls undistinguish'd by the Victor Spade!
65   Thus far both Armies to Belinda yield;
Now to the Baron Fate inclines the Field.
His warlike Amazon her Host invades,
Th' Imperial Consort of the Crown of Spades.
The Club's black Tyrant first her Victim dy'd,
70 Spite of his haughty Mien, and barb'rous Pride:
What boots the Regal Circle on his Head,
His Giant Limbs in State unwieldy spread?
That long behind he trails his pompous Robe,
And of all Monarchs only grasps the Globe?
75   The Baron now his Diamonds pours apace;
Th' embroider'd *King* who shows but half his Face,
And his refulgent *Queen*, with Pow'rs combin'd,
Of broken Troops an easie Conquest find.
Clubs, *Diamonds*, *Hearts*, in wild Disorder seen,
80 With Throngs promiscuous strow the level Green.
Thus when dispers'd a routed Army runs,
Of Asia's Troops, and Africk's Sable Sons,
With like Confusion different Nations fly,
Of various Habit and of various Dye,
85 The pierc'd Battalions dis-united fall,
In Heaps on Heaps; one Fate o'erwhelms them all.
    The *Knave of Diamonds* tries his wily Arts,
And wins (oh shameful Chance!) the *Queen of Hearts*.
At this, the Blood the Virgin's Cheek forsook,

61 *Pam:* Knave of Clubs, which in the game of Loo takes precedence over every other card.

89 *the Blood the Virgin's Cheek forsook:* What worries Belinda is the fact that the Baron has now won four tricks to her four, and if she is still to win she must gain one more.

90   A livid Paleness spreads o'er all her Look;
      She sees, and trembles at th' approaching Ill,
      Just in the Jaws of Ruin, and *Codille*.
      And now, (as oft in some distemper'd State)
      On one nice Trick depends the gen'ral Fate.

95   An *Ace of Hearts* steps forth: The *King* unseen
      Lurk'd in her Hand, and mourn'd his captive *Queen*.
      He springs to Vengeance with an eager pace,
      And falls like Thunder on the prostrate *Ace*.
      The Nymph exulting fills with Shouts the Sky,
100   The Walls, the Woods, and long Canals reply.
          Oh thoughtless Mortals! ever blind to Fate,
      Too soon dejected, and too soon elate!
      Sudden these Honours shall be snatch'd away,
      And curs'd for ever this Victorious Day.

105   For lo! the Board with Cups and Spoons is crown'd,
      The Berries crackle, and the Mill turns round.
      On shining Altars of Japan they raise
      The silver Lamp; the fiery Spirits blaze.
      From silver Spouts the grateful Liquors glide,
110   While China's Earth receives the smoking Tyde.
      At once they gratify their Scent and Taste,
      And frequent Cups prolong the rich Repast.
      Strait hover round the Fair her Airy Band;
      Some, as she sip'd, the fuming Liquor fann'd,
115   Some o'er her Lap their careful Plumes display'd,
      Trembling, and conscious of the rich Brocade.
      Coffee (which makes the Politician wise,
      And see thro' all things with his half-shut Eyes)

92 *Codille:* When either of the Ombre's opponents won he was said to give "codille" to the Ombre.

97-8 *He springs . . . prostrate Ace:* In ombre the status of the red cards when they were not trumps was King, Queen, Knave, Ace. . . . Belinda's King has therefore captured the Baron's Ace.

105 ff. *For lo! the Board, etc.:* a parody of the banquets in epic poetry.

106 *Mill:* coffee-mill.   **107** *Altars of Japan:* japanned (i.e. lacquered) tables.

117 *Politician:* ironically here for the ordinary citizen settling the affairs of the nation in a coffee-house—a favourite haunt for political discussion.

Sent up in Vapours to the Baron's Brain
120 New Stratagems, the radiant Lock to gain.
Ah cease rash Youth! desist ere 'tis too late,
Fear the just Gods, and think of Scylla's Fate!
Chang'd to a Bird, and sent to flit in Air,
She dearly pays for Nisus' injur'd Hair!
125   But when to Mischief Mortals bend their Will,
How soon they find fit Instruments of Ill!
Just then, Clarissa drew with tempting Grace
A two-edg'd Weapon from her shining Case;
So Ladies in Romance assist their Knight,
130 Present the Spear, and arm him for the Fight.
He takes the Gift with rev'rence, and extends
The little Engine on his Fingers' Ends,
This just behind Belinda's Neck he spread,
As o'er the fragrant Steams she bends her Head:
135 Swift to the Lock a thousand Sprights repair,
A thousand Wings, by turns, blow back the Hair,
And thrice they twitch'd the Diamond in her Ear,
Thrice she look'd back, and thrice the Foe drew near.
Just in that instant, anxious Ariel sought
140 The close Recesses of the Virgin's Thought;
As on the Nosegay in her Breast reclin'd,
He watch'd th' Ideas rising in her Mind,
Sudden he view'd, in spite of all her Art,
An Earthly Lover lurking at her Heart.
145 Amaz'd, confus'd, he found his Pow'r expir'd,
Resign'd to Fate, and with a Sigh retir'd.
    The Peer now spreads the glitt'ring Forfex wide,
T'inclose the Lock; now joins it, to divide.

122 *Scylla's Fate:* Scylla betrayed her father Nisus, King of Megara, when his city was besieged by Minos, King of Crete. Knowing that the safety of Megara depended on a single golden hair that grew on the head of Nisus, Scylla, who had fallen in love with Minos, cut it off while her father slept, and gave it to Minos. Minos duly captured Megara, but treated Scylla with contempt. Later she was changed into a bird by the gods.

132 *Engine:* instrument.

147 *Forfex:* the Latin word for a pair of scissors.

Ev'n then, before the fatal Engine clos'd,
150 A wretched Sylph too fondly interpos'd;
Fate urg'd the Sheers, and cut the Sylph in twain,
(But Airy Substance soon unites again)
The meeting Points the sacred Hair dissever
From the fair Head, for ever and for ever!
155   Then flash'd the living Lightning from her Eyes,
And Screams of Horror rend th' affrighted Skies.
Not louder Shrieks to pitying Heav'n are cast,
When Husbands or when Lap-dogs breathe their last,
Or when rich China Vessels, fal'n from high,
160 In glittring Dust and painted Fragments lie!
    Let Wreaths of Triumph now my Temples twine,
(The Victor cry'd) the glorious Prize is mine!
While Fish in Streams, or Birds delight in Air,
Or in a Coach and Six the British Fair,
165 As long as *Atalantis* shall be read,
Or the small Pillow grace a Lady's Bed,
While *Visits* shall be paid on solemn Days,
When numerous Wax-lights in bright Order blaze,
While Nymphs take Treats, or Assignations give,
170 So long my Honour, Name, and Praise shall live!
    What Time wou'd spare, from Steel receives its date,
And Monuments, like Men, submit to Fate!
Steel cou'd the Labour of the Gods destroy,
And strike to Dust th' Imperial Tow'rs of Troy;
175 Steel cou'd the Works of mortal Pride confound,
And hew Triumphal Arches to the Ground.
What Wonder then, fair Nymph! thy Hairs shou'd feel
The conqu'ring Force of unresisted Steel?

163 ff. *While fish in streams, etc.:* The turn of expression (while . . . while . . . so long) is typical of epic poetry.

165 *Atalantis: Secret Memoirs . . . from the New Atalantis,* a volume of scandalous memoirs written by Mrs. Manley (1709).

167 *solemn Days:* those marked by the celebration of religious observances or rites; here used ironically for the days in the month when a fashionable lady received visitors.

169 *Treats:* Cf. i, 96.   **171** *date:* end.

CANTO IV

But anxious Cares the pensive Nymph opprest,
And secret Passions labour'd in her Breast.
Not youthful Kings in Battel seiz'd alive,
Not scornful Virgins who their Charms survive,
5 Not ardent Lovers robb'd of all their Bliss,
Not ancient Ladies when refus'd a Kiss,
Not Tyrants fierce that unrepenting die,
Not Cynthia when her Manteau's pinn'd awry,
E'er felt such Rage, Resentment and Despair,
10 As Thou, sad Virgin! for thy ravish'd Hair.
    For, that sad moment, when the Sylphs withdrew,
And Ariel weeping from Belinda flew,
Umbriel, a dusky melancholy Spright,
As ever sully'd the fair face of Light,
15 Down to the Central Earth, his proper Scene,
Repair'd to search the gloomy Cave of Spleen.
    Swift on his sooty Pinions flitts the Gnome,
And in a Vapour reach'd the dismal Dome.
No cheerful Breeze this sullen Region knows,
20 The dreaded East is all the Wind that blows.
Here, in a Grotto, sheltred close from Air,
And screen'd in Shades from Day's detested Glare,
She sighs for ever on her pensive Bed,
Pain at her Side, and Megrim at her Head.
25   Two Handmaids wait the Throne: Alike in Place,
But diff'ring far in Figure and in Face.
Here stood Ill-nature like an ancient Maid,
Her wrinkled Form in Black and White array'd;

8 *Manteau:* cloak.

15 *Down to the Central Earth:* another epic feature, the journey to the underworld.

16 *Spleen:* the fashionable malady of the period, hard to define and loosely applied to low spirits of a hypochondriac nature.

18 *Vapour:* Pope is punning on this word, which in the plural form had much the same meaning as spleen. Cf. l. 59.

24 *Megrim:* migraine, headache.

With store of Pray'rs, for Mornings, Nights, and Noons,
30   Her Hand is fill'd; her Bosom with Lampoons.
     There Affectation with a sickly Mien
Shows in her Cheek the Roses of Eighteen,
Practis'd to Lisp, and hang the Head aside,
Faints into Airs, and languishes with Pride;
35   On the rich Quilt sinks with becoming Woe,
Wrapt in a Gown, for Sickness, and for Show.
The Fair-ones feel such Maladies as these,
When each new Night-Dress gives a new Disease.
     A constant Vapour o'er the Palace flies;
40   Strange Phantoms rising as the Mists arise;
Dreadful, as Hermit's Dreams in haunted Shades,
Or bright as Visions of expiring Maids.
Now glaring Fiends, and Snakes on rolling Spires,
Pale Spectres, gaping Tombs, and Purple Fires:
45   Now Lakes of liquid Gold, Elysian Scenes,
And Crystal Domes, and Angels in Machines.
     Unnumber'd Throngs on ev'ry side are seen
Of Bodies chang'd to various Forms by Spleen.
Here living Teapots stand, one Arm held out,
50   One bent; the Handle this, and that the Spout:
A Pipkin there like Homer's Tripod walks;
Here sighs a Jar, and there a Goose-pye talks;
Men prove with Child, as pow'rful Fancy works,
And Maids turn'd Bottels, call aloud for Corks.

36 *for Sickness, and for Show:* i.e. Affectation, having got a new night-dress in which to display her charms, takes to her bed to receive her visitors.

43 *Spires:* coils.

44 *purple:* blood-red.

47 ff. *Unnumber'd Throngs, etc.:* Pope describes a number of the illusions induced by the spleen. To the word "Goose-pye" (l. 52) he adds the note: "Alludes to a real fact, a Lady of distinction imagin'd herself in this condition."

51 *Homer's Tripod walks:* Homer tells how Vulcan made twenty tripods that would move about as he willed (*Iliad*, xviii).

53 *Men prove with Child:* A certain Dr. Edward Pelling (d. 1718), a royal chaplain, believed himself to be in this condition.

55   Safe past the Gnome thro' this fantastick Band,
    A Branch of healing Spleenwort in his hand.
    Then thus addrest the Pow'r—Hail wayward Queen!
    Who rule the Sex to Fifty from Fifteen,
    Parent of Vapours and of Female Wit,
60   Who give th' Hysteric or Poetic Fit,
    On various Tempers act by various ways,
    Make some take Physick, others scribble Plays;
    Who cause the Proud their Visits to delay,
    And send the Godly in a Pett, to pray.
65   A Nymph there is, that all thy Pow'r disdains,
    And thousands more in equal Mirth maintains.
    But oh! if e'er thy Gnome could spoil a Grace,
    Or raise a Pimple on a beauteous Face,
    Like Citron-Waters Matrons' Cheeks inflame,
70   Or change Complexions at a losing Game;
    If e'er with airy Horns I planted Heads,
    Or rumpled Petticoats, or tumbled Beds,
    Or caus'd Suspicion when no Soul was rude,
    Or discompos'd the Head-dress of a Prude,
75   Or e'er to costive Lap-Dog gave Disease,
    Which not the Tears of brightest Eyes could ease:
    Hear me, and touch Belinda with Chagrin;
    That single Act gives half the World the Spleen.
      The Goddess with a discontented Air
80   Seems to reject him, tho' she grants his Pray'r.
    A wondrous Bag with both her Hands she binds,
    Like that where once Ulysses held the Winds;
    There she collects the Force of Female Lungs,
    Sighs, Sobs, and Passions, and the War of Tongues.
85   A Vial next she fills with fainting Fears,
    Soft Sorrows, melting Griefs, and flowing Tears.

56 *Spleenwort:* a fern sometimes used to counteract the spleen.

69 *Citron-Waters:* brandy flavoured with lemon.

71 *airy Horns:* imaginary horns, worn (according to the old joke) by cuckolds.

82 *Ulysses held the Winds:* Homer (*Iliad*, x) tells how Aeolus gave Ulysses the adverse winds tied up in leather bags.

The Gnome rejoicing bears her Gifts away,
Spreads his black Wings, and slowly mounts to Day.
   Sunk in Thalestris' Arms the Nymph he found,
90   Her Eyes dejected and her Hair unbound.
Full o'er their Heads the swelling Bag he rent,
And all the Furies issued at the Vent.
Belinda burns with more than mortal Ire,
And fierce Thalestris fans the rising Fire.
95   O wretched Maid! she spread her Hands, and cry'd,
(While Hampton's Ecchoes, wretched Maid! reply'd)
Was it for this you took such constant Care
The Bodkin, Comb, and Essence to prepare;
For this your Locks in Paper-Durance bound,
100 For this with tort'ring Irons wreath'd around?
For this with Fillets strain'd your tender Head,
And bravely bore the double Loads of Lead?
Gods! shall the Ravisher display your Hair,
While the Fops envy, and the Ladies stare!
105 Honour forbid! at whose unrival'd Shrine
Ease, Pleasure, Virtue, All, our Sex resign.
Methinks already I your Tears survey,
Already hear the horrid things they say,
Already see you a degraded Toast,
110 And all your Honour in a Whisper lost!
How shall I, then, your helpless Fame defend?
'Twill then be Infamy to seem your Friend!
And shall this Prize, th' inestimable Prize,
Expos'd thro' Crystal to the gazing Eyes,

---

94 *fierce Thalestris:* She is fierce because she bears the same name as an ancient Queen of the Amazons.

98 *Bodkin:* an ornament for the hair. Cf. v, 95.

99 *Paper-Durance:* i.e. curl-papers.

100 *Irons:* curling irons.

105 *Honour:* reputation, keeping up appearances.

109 *a degraded Toast:* a woman whose health is drunk with a knowing wink of the eye.

114 f. *Expos'd thro' Crystal, etc.:* The Baron will wear a ring enclosing a wisp of Belinda's hair and set with diamonds.

115 And heighten'd by the Diamond's circling Rays,
    On that Rapacious Hand for ever blaze?
    Sooner shall Grass in Hide-Park Circus grow,
    And Wits take Lodgings in the Sound of Bow;
    Sooner let Earth, Air, Sea, to Chaos fall,
120 Men, Monkies, Lap-dogs, Parrots, perish all!
        She said; then raging to Sir Plume repairs,
    And bids her *Beau* demand the precious Hairs:
    (Sir Plume, of Amber Snuff-box justly vain,
    And the nice Conduct of a clouded Cane)
125 With earnest Eyes, and round unthinking Face,
    He first the Snuff-box open'd, then the Case,
    And thus broke out—'My Lord, why, what the Devil?
    Z—ds! damn the Lock! 'fore Gad, you must be civil!
    Plague on't! 'tis past a Jest—nay prithee, Pox!
130 Give her the Hair'—he spoke, and rapp'd his Box.
        It grieves me much (reply'd the Peer again)
    Who speaks so well shou'd ever speak in vain.
    But by this Lock, this sacred Lock I swear,
    (Which never more shall join its parted Hair,
135 Which never more its Honours shall renew,
    Clipt from the lovely Head where late it grew)

117 *Hide-Park Circus:* better known as the Ring (cf. i, 44). Since Pope
has just mentioned the Baron's ring he is driven to avoid the use of the word
again here.

118 *in the Sound of Bow:* The citizens or "cits" lived "within the sound of
Bow bells": the polite end of the town was Westminster and the new
streets west of what is now Piccadilly Circus. (For the construction
"Sooner . . . sooner", cf. iii, 163 ff.)

120 *Monkies, Lap-dogs, Parrots:* all fashionable pets in Queen Anne's day.
121 *Sir Plume:* Sir George Browne, a baronet, second cousin to Arabella
Fermor.

123 f. *Snuff-box . . . Cane:* essential parts of a beau's equipment.
clouded: diversified with irregular patches of colour in the amber or bone
handle.

126 *open'd:* Pope is punning on this word: when a counsel at law states
the grounds on which he will plead he is said to "open" his case.
128 *Z—ds!:* Zounds (God's wounds).
135 *Honours:* graces, adornments. Cf. also 140.

That while my Nostrils draw the vital Air,
This Hand, which won it, shall for ever wear.
He spoke, and speaking, in proud Triumph spread
140   The long-contended Honours of her Head.
    But Umbriel, hateful Gnome! forbears not so;
He breaks the Vial whence the Sorrows flow.
Then see! the Nymph in beauteous Grief appears,
Her Eyes half-languishing, half-drown'd in Tears;
145   On her heav'd Bosom hung her drooping Head,
Which, with a Sigh, she rais'd; and thus she said.
    For ever curs'd be this detested Day,
Which snatch'd my best, my fav'rite Curl away!
Happy! ah ten times happy, had I been,
150   If Hampton Court these Eyes had never seen!
Yet am not I the first mistaken Maid,
By Love of Courts to num'rous Ills betray'd.
Oh had I rather un-admir'd remain'd
In some lone Isle, or distant Northern Land;
155   Where the gilt Chariot never marks the Way,
Where none learn Ombre, none e'er taste *Bohea!*
There kept my Charms conceal'd from mortal Eye,
Like Roses that in Desarts bloom and die.
What mov'd my Mind with youthful Lords to rome?
160   O had I stay'd, and said my Pray'rs at home!
'Twas this, the Morning Omens seem'd to tell;
Thrice from my trembling hand the Patch-box fell;
The tott'ring China shook without a Wind,
Nay, Poll sate mute, and *Shock* was most Unkind!
165   A Sylph too warn'd me of the Threats of Fate,
In mystic Visions, now believ'd too late!
See the poor Remnants of these slighted Hairs!
My hands shall rend what ev'n thy Rapine spares:

155 *Chariot:* a light four-wheeled carriage (pronounced "charrit").

156 *Bohea:* a species of tea.

158 *Like Roses, etc.:* The thought is borrowed from Waller's "Go, lovely rose", ll. 8-10.

162 *Patch-box:* a box for holding the "patches" mentioned at i, 138.

170 These, in two sable Ringlets taught to break,
      Once gave new Beauties to the snowie Neck.
      The Sister-Lock now sits uncouth, alone,
      And in its Fellow's Fate foresees its own;
      Uncurl'd it hangs, the fatal Sheers demands;
      And tempts once more thy sacrilegious Hands.
175 Oh hadst thou, Cruel! been content to seize
      Hairs less in sight, or any Hairs but these!

CANTO V

      She said: the pitying Audience melt in Tears,
      But Fate and Jove had stopp'd the Baron's Ears.
      In vain Thalestris with Reproach assails,
      For who can move when fair Belinda fails?
5   Not half so fixt the Trojan cou'd remain,
      While Anna begg'd and Dido rag'd in vain.
      Then grave *Clarissa* graceful wav'd her Fan;
      Silence ensu'd, and thus the Nymph began.
        Say, why are Beauties prais'd and honour'd most,
10 The wise Man's Passion, and the vain Man's Toast?
      Why deck'd with all that Land and Sea afford,
      Why Angels call'd, and Angel-like ador'd?
      Why round our Coaches crowd the white-glov'd Beaus,
      Why bows the Side-box from its inmost Rows?
15 How vain are all these Glories, all our Pains,
      Unless good Sense preserve what Beauty gains:
      That Men may say, when we the Front-box grace,
      Behold the first in Virtue, as in Face!
      Oh! if to dance all Night, and dress all Day,
20 Charm'd the Small-pox, or chas'd old Age away;
      Who would not scorn what Huswife's Cares produce,

5 f. *Trojan . . . Anna . . . Dido:* After the fall of Troy Aeneas arrived at Carthage. Dido the Queen fell in love with him, and begged him to stay, but the pleas of Dido and her sister Anna were in vain.

9 ff. *Say, why are Beauties, etc.:* Clarissa's speech parodies that of Sarpedon to Glaucus in *Iliad*, xii.

14, 17 *Side-box . . . Front-box:* boxes at the theatre.

Or who would learn one earthly Thing of Use?
To patch, nay ogle, might become a Saint,
Nor could it sure be such a Sin to paint.
25 But since, alas! frail Beauty must decay,
Curl'd or uncurl'd, since Locks will turn to grey,
Since painted, or not painted, all shall fade,
And she who scorns a Man, must die a Maid;
What then remains, but well our Pow'r to use,
30 And keep good Humour still whate'er we lose?
And trust me, Dear! good Humour can prevail,
When Airs, and Flights, and Screams, and Scolding fail.
Beauties in vain their pretty Eyes may roll;
Charms strike the Sight, but Merit wins the Soul.
35   So spoke the Dame, but no Applause ensu'd;
Belinda frown'd, Thalestris call'd her Prude.
To Arms, to Arms! the fierce Virago cries,
And swift as Lightning to the Combate flies.
All side in Parties, and begin th' Attack;
40 Fans clap, Silks russle, and tough Whalebones crack;
Heroes' and Heroins' Shouts confus'dly rise,
And base, and treble Voices strike the Skies.
No common Weapons in their Hands are found,
Like Gods they fight, nor dread a mortal Wound.
45   So when bold Homer makes the Gods engage,
And heav'nly Breasts with human Passions rage;
'Gainst Pallas, Mars; Latona, Hermes arms;
And all Olympus rings with loud Alarms.
Jove's Thunder roars, Heav'n trembles all around;
50 Blue Neptune storms, the bellowing Deeps resound;
Earth shakes her nodding Tow'rs, the Ground gives way;
And the pale Ghosts start at the Flash of Day!
Triumphant Umbriel on a Sconce's Height
Clapt his glad Wings, and sate to view the Fight:
55 Propt on their Bodkin Spears, the Sprights survey
The growing Combat, or assist the Fray.

45 *the Gods engage:* See *Iliad,* xx, 91 ff.
53 *a Sconce's Height:* A sconce was a candlestick bracket fastened to a wall.

While thro' the Press enrag'd Thalestris flies,
And scatters Deaths around from both her Eyes,
A Beau and Witling perish'd in the Throng,
60 One dy'd in Metaphor, and one in Song.
O cruel Nymph! a living Death I bear,
Cry'd Dapperwit, and sunk beside his Chair.
A mournful Glance Sir Fopling upwards cast,
Those Eyes are made so killing—was his last:
65 Thus on Meander's flow'ry Margin lies
Th' expiring Swan, and as he sings he dies.
    When bold Sir Plume had drawn Clarissa down,
Chloe stept in, and kill'd him with a Frown;
She smil'd to see the doughty Hero slain,
70 But at her Smile, the Beau reviv'd again.
    Now Jove suspends his golden Scales in Air,
Weighs the Men's Wits against the Lady's Hair;
The doubtful Beam long nods from side to side;
At length the Wits mount up, the Hairs subside.
75   See fierce Belinda on the Baron flies,
With more than usual Lightning in her Eyes;
Nor fear'd the Chief th' unequal Fight to try,
Who sought no more than on his Foe to die.
But this bold Lord, with manly Strength indu'd,
80 She with one Finger and a Thumb subdu'd:
Just where the Breath of Life his Nostrils drew,
A Charge of Snuff the wily Virgin threw;
The Gnomes direct, to ev'ry Atome just,
The pungent Grains of titillating Dust.
85 Sudden, with starting Tears each Eye o'erflows,
And the high Dome re-ecchoes to his Nose.
    Now meet thy Fate, incens'd Belinda cry'd,
And drew a deadly Bodkin from her Side.
(The same, his ancient Personage to deck,
90 Her great great Grandsire wore about his Neck
In three Seal-Rings; which after, melted down,

---

64 "*Those Eyes are made so killing*": the opening words of a popular song in Buononcini's opera *Camilla*, which opened in London in 1706.

Form'd a vast Buckle for his Widow's Gown:
Her infant Grandame's Whistle next it grew,
The Bells she gingled, and the Whistle blew;
95 Then in a Bodkin grac'd her Mother's Hairs,
Which long she wore, and now Belinda wears.)
    Boast not my Fall (he cry'd) insulting Foe!
Thou by some other shalt be laid as low.
Nor think, to die dejects my lofty Mind;
100 All that I dread, is leaving you behind!
Rather than so, ah let me still survive,
And burn in Cupid's Flames,—but burn alive.
    Restore the Lock! she cries; and all around
Restore the Lock! the vaulted Roofs rebound.
105 Not fierce Othello in so loud a Strain
Roar'd for the Handkerchief that caus'd his Pain.
But see how oft Ambitious Aims are cross'd,
And Chiefs contend 'till all the Prize is lost!
The Lock, obtain'd with Guilt, and kept with Pain,
110 In ev'ry place is sought, but sought in vain:
With such a Prize no Mortal must be blest,
So Heav'n decrees! with Heav'n who can contest?
    Some thought it mounted to the Lunar Sphere,
Since all things lost on Earth, are treasur'd there.
115 There Heroes' Wits are kept in pondrous Vases,
And Beaus' in Snuff-boxes and Tweezer-Cases.
There broken Vows, and Death-bed Alms are found,
And Lovers' Hearts with Ends of Riband bound;
The Courtier's Promises, and Sick Man's Pray'rs,
120 The Smiles of Harlots, and the Tears of Heirs,
Cages for Gnats, and Chains to Yoak a Flea;
Dry'd Butterflies, and Tomes of Casuistry.
    But trust the Muse—she saw it upward rise,
Tho' mark'd by none but quick Poetic Eyes:

105 *Othello:* See *Othello*, iv, i.

113-22 This passage is based on Ariosto's *Orlando Furioso*, canto xxxiv, where Astolfo journeys to the moon in search of Orlando's lost wits.

122 *Tomes of Casuistry:* books resolving cases of conscience.

125 (So Rome's great Founder to the Heav'ns withdrew,
    To Proculus alone confess'd in view.)
    A sudden Star, it shot thro' liquid Air,
    And drew behind a radiant Trail of Hair.
    Not Berenice's Locks first rose so bright,
130 The Heav'ns bespangling with dishevel'd Light.
    The Sylphs behold it kindling as it flies,
    And pleas'd pursue its Progress thro' the Skies.
      This the Beau-monde shall from the Mall survey,
    And hail with Musick its propitious Ray.
135 This, the blest Lover shall for Venus take,
    And send up Vows from Rosamonda's Lake.
    This Partridge soon shall view in cloudless Skies,
    When next he looks thro' Galilæo's Eyes;
    And hence th' Egregious Wizard shall foredoom
140 The Fate of Louis, and the Fall of Rome,
      Then cease, bright Nymph! to mourn thy ravish'd Hair
    Which adds new Glory to the shining Sphere!
    Not all the Tresses that fair Head can boast
    Shall draw such Envy as the Lock you lost.

126 *Proculus:* a Roman who claimed that Romulus had appeared to him after his death in more than human form.

127 *liquid:* clear.

129 *Berenice's Locks:* Berenice vowed that if her husband should return safely from an expedition she would give Venus all her hair. Some time after his safe return, her locks, which had been placed in the temple of Venus, disappeared, and it was said that they had become a constellation.

133 *the Mall:* a fashionable walk in St. James's Park.

136 *Rosamonda's Lake:* Rosamond's Pond in St. James's Park, a favourite haunt of courting couples.

137 *Partridge:* John Partridge, a well-known astrologer who published almanacs. He had recently been ridiculed by Swift in his *Predictions . . . by Isaac Bickerstaff*, 1708.

138 *Galilæo's Eyes:* Galileo did not invent the telescope, but greatly improved it.

140 *Louis:* Louis XIV. In 1712, when the first version of the poem appeared, the fate of Louis was of considerable importance since England and France were at war.

145 For, after all the Murders of your Eye,
When, after Millions slain, your self shall die;
When those fair Suns shall sett, as sett they must,
And all those Tresses shall be laid in Dust;
This Lock, the Muse shall consecrate to Fame,
150 And mid'st the Stars inscribe Belinda's Name!

PROLOGUE DESIGN'D FOR MR. DURFY'S LAST PLAY

TOM D'URFEY (1653-1723) had been a successful playwright in the days of Charles II, but by the time this prologue was written he was an elderly man in reduced circumstances. In June 1713 a benefit performance of one of his early comedies was put on, and it may have been for this occasion that the prologue was written—although whether it was ever spoken is another matter. The prologue first appeared in Steele's *Poetical Miscellanies*, 1714, when it was said to have been "Written by several Hands". It may, therefore, be a joint composition, but it was republished in Pope's and Swift's *Miscellanies*, *The Last Volume*, 1727, and it certainly has some unmistakable signs of Pope's composition. Pope was quite capable of doing a kindness to D'Urfey, but equally capable of doing it with a certain amount of witty *double entendre*; e.g. "But ever writ, as none e'er writ before", and "Nor sinks his Credit lower than it was".

Grown old in Rhyme, 'twere barbarous to discard
Your persevering, unexhausted Bard:
Damnation follows Death in other Men,
But your damn'd Poet lives and writes again.
5 Th' advent'rous Lover is successful still,
Who strives to please the Fair *against her Will*:
Be kind, and make him in his Wishes easy,
Who in your own *Despite* has strove to please ye.
He scorn'd to borrow from the Wits of yore;
10 But ever writ, as none e'er writ before.
You modern Wits, should each Man bring his Claim,
Have desperate Debentures on your Fame;

12 *Debentures:* debts. The metaphor is sustained in "Fund" (l. 15) and "Credit" (l. 16), where there is also a play on the word.

And little wou'd be left you, I'm afraid,
If all your Debts to Greece and Rome were paid.
15 From his deep Fund our Author largely draws;
Nor sinks his Credit lower than it was.
Tho' Plays for Honour in old Time he made,
'Tis now for better Reasons—to be paid.
Believe him, he has known the World too long,
20 And seen the Death of much Immortal Song.
He says, poor Poets lost, while Players won,
As Pimps grow rich, while Gallants are undone.
Tho' Tom the Poet writ with Ease and Pleasure,
The Comick Tom abounds in other Treasure.
25 Fame is at best an unperforming Cheat;
But 'tis substantial Happiness to *eat*—
Let Ease, his last Request, be of your giving,
Nor force him to be damn'd, to get his Living.

21 *while Players won:* i.e. the actors, not the authors, have been the gainers.

23 *Tom the Poet:* D'Urfey was a famous song-writer.

24 *The Comick Tom* was the writer of comedies.

28 *Nor force him to be damn'd, etc.:* i.e. Do not force him to write more plays (which will inevitably be damned) to get a living.

EPISTLE TO MISS BLOUNT, ON HER LEAVING THE TOWN, AFTER THE CORONATION

THIS beautiful poem is an example of the familiar epistle so frequently found in eighteenth-century poetry. Among Pope's friends were Teresa and Martha Blount of Mapledurham, who, like himself, were Roman Catholics. The epistle is addressed to Teresa (who certainly attracted Pope at this time, but from whom he later became estranged), and the coronation she failed to see was that of George I, in October, 1714. Pope writes from the Town in the gay, urbane tradition of the wit, laughing at the dull, uneventful life of the country (complete with a visit from the Squire); but much of the peculiar effect of the poem lies in the undertone of feeling. The easy satire of the first half gives way at l. 31 ("In some fair evening, on your elbow laid . . .") to a gentler passage, marked by such words and phrases as "dream", "pensive", "closing eyes", and carried along on a more

measured and dream-like rhythm. This is quickly dissipated when Zephalinda gives "one flirt" to her fan, but it half returns at l. 41, only to be
interrupted a second time when Gay pats the poet's shoulder. The poem
ends, however, half-way between the two worlds of satire and sentiment.
As an exercise in emotional ambivalence—showing feeling in public without showing it too much—it is a small triumph of tone.

As some fond virgin, whom her mother's care
Drags from the town to wholsom country air,
Just when she learns to roll a melting eye,
And hear a spark, yet think no danger nigh;
5   From the dear man unwilling she must sever,
Yet takes one kiss before she parts for ever:
Thus from the world fair Zephalinda flew,
Saw others happy, and with sighs withdrew;
Not that their pleasures caus'd her discontent,
10 She sigh'd not that They stay'd, but that She went.
    She went, to plain-work, and to purling brooks,
Old-fashion'd halls, dull aunts, and croaking rooks,
She went from Op'ra, park, assembly, play,
To morning walks, and pray'rs three hours a day;
15 To pass her time 'twixt reading and Bohea,
To muse, and spill her solitary tea,
Or o'er cold coffee trifle with the spoon,
Count the slow clock, and dine exact at noon;
Divert her eyes with pictures in the fire,
20 Hum half a tune, tell stories to the squire;
Up to her godly garret after sev'n,
There starve and pray, for that's the way to heav'n.
    Some Squire, perhaps, you take delight to rack;
Whose game is Whisk, whose treat a toast in sack,
25 Who visits with a gun, presents you birds,
Then gives a smacking buss, and cries—No words!
Or with his hounds comes hollowing from the stable,
Makes love with nods, and knees beneath a table;

4 *spark:* beau.
7 *Zephalinda:* a pen-name used by Teresa Blount.
11 *plain-work:* sewing.   13 *park:* either St. James's Park or Hyde Park.
24 *Whisk:* whist.   *treat:* entertainment.   26 *buss:* kiss.

Whose laughs are hearty, tho' his jests are coarse,
30 And loves you best of all things—but his horse.
　　In some fair evening, on your elbow laid,
You dream of triumphs in the rural shade;
In pensive thoughts recall the fancy'd scene,
See Coronations rise on ev'ry green;
35 Before you pass th' imaginary sights
Of Lords, and Earls, and Dukes, and garter'd Knights;
While the spread Fan o'ershades your closing eyes;
Then give one flirt, and all the vision flies.
Thus vanish sceptres, coronets, and balls,
40 And leave you in lone woods, or empty walls.
　　So when your slave, at some dear, idle time,
(Not plagu'd with headachs, or the want of rhime)
Stands in the streets, abstracted from the crew,
And while he seems to study, thinks of you:
45 Just when his fancy points your sprightly eyes,
Or sees the blush of Parthenissa rise,
Gay pats my shoulder, and you vanish quite;
Streets, chairs, and coxcombs rush upon my sight;
Vext to be still in town, I knit my brow,
50 Look sow'r, and hum a song—as you may now.

32 *triumphs:* public festivities.
36 *garter'd Knights:* i.e. Knights of the Order of the Garter.
45 *points:* perhaps as a spaniel or a pointer "points" game.
46 *Parthenissa:* Martha Blount.

ELEGY TO THE MEMORY OF AN
UNFORTUNATE LADY

THE elegy was a literary "kind" of some importance in classical poetry, and is well represented in the work of Ovid, Propertius and Tibullus. Pope, who liked to try his hand at different kinds of poetry, was quite capable of writing an elegy for the sake of writing an elegy. The question therefore is, Did the form come first on this occasion and the subject-matter later, or was Pope so concerned about the sad fate of some particular eighteenth-century young woman that he felt compelled to find expression for it and for his own feelings about it? In his own day it was widely believed that his Elegy commemorated an actual tragedy in private life, and no doubt the ensuing mystery helped to account for the great interest shown in this poem. Several candidates were proposed; but, so far as is known, Pope never committed himself to identifying the unfortunate lady, and the lines—

> How lov'd, how honour'd once, avails thee not,
> To whom related, or by whom begot—

seem to indicate that he would have deprecated any such attempt. If, as Johnson and others have supposed, the poem recalls the fate of a lovesick and desperate girl whose guardian forbade her to marry the man of her choice, such a situation (abating the suicide) must have been frequent enough in a century in which arranged marriages were the common practice among the upper classes. In this poem Pope offended the moral sense of Dr. Johnson by "the illaudable singularity of treating suicide with respect", but this too was common form among eighteenth-century writers: in the highly successful tragedy, *The Fair Penitent* (1703), by Pope's friend Nicholas Rowe, Calista stabs herself in the fifth act and expires in a blaze of tragic glory. Although the "Elegy" is now something of a period piece, it is still, with its carefully chiselled language and its balanced expression of public mourning, an impressive literary monument—even although the monument is in all probability a cenotaph.

> What beck'ning ghost, along the moonlight shade
> Invites my step, and points to yonder glade?
> 'Tis she!—but why that bleeding bosom gor'd,
> Why dimly gleams the visionary sword?
> 5 Oh ever beauteous, ever friendly! tell,
> Is it, in heav'n, a crime to love too well?
> To bear too tender, or too firm a heart,
> To act a Lover's or a *Roman's* part?
> Is there no bright reversion in the sky,
> 10 For those who greatly think, or bravely die?
> Why bade ye else, ye Pow'rs! her soul aspire
> Above the vulgar flight of low desire?

1 *beck'ning:* A mystery is suggested with the opening words of the poem: the ghost has something to impart.

8 *a Roman's part:* Cf. Shakespeare's *Antony and Cleopatra*. When Cleopatra has resolved upon suicide she says she will do "what's brave, what's noble . . . after the high Roman fashion".

8 *reversion in the sky:* i.e. the right of inheriting a place in heaven.

Ambition first sprung from your blest abodes;
The glorious fault of Angels and of Gods:
15 Thence to their Images on earth it flows,
And in the breasts of Kings and Heroes glows!
Most souls, 'tis true, but peep out once an age,
Dull sullen pris'ners in the body's cage:
Dim lights of life that burn a length of years,
20 Useless, unseen, as lamps in sepulchres;
Like Eastern Kings a lazy state they keep,
And close confin'd to their own palace sleep.
    From these perhaps (ere nature bade her die)
Fate snatch'd her early to the pitying sky.
25 As into air the purer spirits flow,
And sep'rate from their kindred dregs below;
So flew the soul to its congenial place,
Nor left one virtue to redeem her Race.
    But thou, false guardian of a charge too good,
30 Thou, mean deserter of thy brother's blood!
See on these ruby lips the trembling breath,
These cheeks, now fading at the blast of death;
Cold is that breast which warm'd the world before,
And those love-darting eyes must roll no more.
35 Thus, if eternal justice rules the ball,
Thus shall your wives, and thus your children fall:
On all the line a sudden vengeance waits,
And frequent herses shall besiege your gates.
There passengers shall stand, and pointing say,
40 (While the long fun'rals blacken all the way)

13-14 *Ambition . . . The glorious fault:* This thought is frequent in the poets. Cf. Shakespeare, *Henry VIII*, III. ii. 441, and Dryden, *Absalom and Achitophel*, l. 372, where ambition is called "a godlike sin".

25 *purer spirits:* as in a chemical experiment: "spirits" here is a kind of pun, as is "kindred" in the next line.

28 *Nor . . . Race:* an imitation of Juvenal, *Sat.* iv, 2 f. *race* = family.

34 *love-darting eyes:* from Milton, *Comus*, 753.

39 *passengers:* wayfarers, passers by.

40 *long fun'rals:* Upper-class funerals in the eighteenth century were elaborate, with a long procession of mourning coaches.

Lo these were they, whose souls the Furies steel'd,
And curs'd with hearts unknowing how to yield.
Thus unlamented pass the proud away,
The gaze of fools, and pageant of a day.
45 So perish all, whose breast ne'er learn'd to glow
For others' good, or melt at others' woe.
    What can atone (oh ever injur'd shade!)
Thy fate unpity'd, and thy rites unpaid?
No friend's complaint, no kind domestic tear
50 Pleas'd thy pale ghost, or grac'd thy mournful bier;
By foreign hands thy dying eyes were clos'd,
By foreign hands thy decent limbs compos'd,
By foreign hands thy humble grave adorn'd,
By strangers honour'd, and by strangers mourn'd!
55 What tho' no friends in sable weeds appear,
Grieve for an hour, perhaps, then mourn a year,
And bear about the mockery of woe
To midnight dances, and the publick show?
What tho' no weeping Loves thy ashes grace,
60 Nor polish'd marble emulate thy face?
What tho' no sacred earth allow thee room,
Nor hallow'd dirge be mutter'd o'er thy tomb?
Yet shall thy grave with rising flow'rs be drest,
And the green turf lie lightly on thy breast:
65 There shall the morn her earliest tears bestow,
There the first roses of the year shall blow;
While Angels with their silver wings o'ershade
The ground, now sacred by thy reliques made.
    So peaceful rests, without a stone, a name,
70 What once had beauty, titles, wealth, and fame.

41-2 *Lo . . . yield:* When the "Elegy" was written Pope was still at work on his translation of the *Iliad*. Those two lines recall his translation of *Iliad*, xxii, 447-8. Similarly, ll. 45-6 recall his translation of *Odyssey*, xviii, 269-70).

49 *complaint:* lamentation.   **56** *mourn:* i.e. wear mourning.

59 *weeping Loves:* as in eighteenth-century funeral monuments.

61 *no sacred earth:* Suicides could not be buried in hallowed ground.

65 *earliest tears:* dew drops.

How lov'd, how honour'd once, avails thee not,
To whom related, or by whom begot;
A heap of dust alone remains of thee;
'Tis all thou art, and all the proud shall be!
75   Poets themselves must fall, like those they sung;
Deaf the prais'd ear, and mute the tuneful tongue.
Ev'n he, whose soul now melts in mournful lays,
Shall shortly want the gen'rous tear he pays;
Then from his closing eyes thy form shall part,
80   And the last pangs shall tear thee from his heart,
Life's idle bus'ness at one gasp be o'er,
The Muse forgot, and thou belov'd no more!

78 *want:* either (*a*) be without, lack, or (*b*) need.

FRAGMENT OF A SATIRE

THE following lines were published in *Miscellanies, The Last Volume*, 1727.
They had first appeared in a shortened version (the six lines on Gildon and
Dennis, followed by the character of Addison) in *The St. James's Journal*,
December 15, 1722. Gildon and Dennis had been attacking Pope in print
for a number of years. The relations between Pope and Addison are more
complicated; but Pope believed, probably with justification, that Addison
had encouraged Thomas Tickell to produce and publish a translation of
The Iliad, Book I, when Pope's own translation of Homer, already
announced, was due to appear. Other grievances and perhaps misunder-
standings accumulated, and some time after May 1716 Pope sent Addison
the first sketch of his famous character, with a veiled threat to publish it if
Addison continued to carry on what Pope obviously believed to be a private
vendetta. According to Pope's account of the matter, Addison, who was
sixteen years his senior and who died in 1719, "used [him] very civilly
ever after". When he published the expanded version in 1727 Pope took
the opportunity of paying off a few other scores, especially attacking
critics like Theobald, who had exposed errors and omissions in his
edition of Shakespeare (1725). Finally, in 1734, he incorporated the whole
piece with a few minor revisions in his *Epistle to Dr. Arbuthnot*. The lines
on Addison are an example of deadly personal satire, but they are also an
example of a form of writing in which Pope excelled—the character. Even
if Addison were *not* he, we should still recognise the type of denigrating
critic, jealous of a rival writer and yet afraid to come out into the open, a
master of casual innuendo and the indirect statement. The text is from *The
Works*, Vol. II. Part ii (1738).

> If meagre Gildon draws his venal Quill,
> I wish the Man a Dinner, and sit still.
> If dreadful Dennis raves in furious Fret,
> I'll answer Dennis when I am in Debt.
> 5   'Tis Hunger, and not Malice, makes them print,
> And who'll wage War with Bedlam or the Mint?
>   Should some more sober Criticks come abroad,
> If wrong, I smile; if right, I kiss the Rod.
> Pains, Reading, Study, are their just Pretence,
> 10   And all they want is Spirit, Taste, and Sense.
> Commas and Points they set exactly right;
> And 'twere a Sin to rob them of their *Mite*.
> Yet ne'er one Sprig of Laurel grac'd those Ribbalds,
> From slashing B[entle]y down to pidling Tibbalds:
> 15   Who thinks he *reads* when he but *scans* and *spells*,
> A Word-catcher, that lives on Syllables.
> Yet ev'n this Creature may some Notice claim,
> Wrapt round and sanctify'd with Shakespear's Name;
> Pretty, in Amber, to observe the forms

1 *Gildon:* Charles Gildon (1665-1724), a miscellaneous writer, first sneered at Pope in a critical piece called *The New Rehearsal* (1714), and followed this by further attacks.

3 *Dennis:* Pope had offended John Dennis (1657-1734) by laughing at him in *An Essay on Criticism* (1711), and Dennis repaid this offence by frequent and emphatic criticisms of his poems as they appeared.

4 *when I am in Debt:* i.e. as Dennis now is. The second "I" takes the emphasis.

6 *Bedlam:* the hospital of St. Bethlehem, a lunatic asylum.   *the Mint:* a sanctuary for debtors in Southwark.

9 *just Pretence:* what they can fairly lay claim to.

14 *slashing B[entle]y:* Richard Bentley, the famous classical scholar. He had offended Pope by not admiring his translation of Homer. The "slashing" has particular reference to his wild emendations in his edition of *Paradise Lost* (1732).   *pidling Tibbalds:* trifling Theobald; i.e. Lewis Theobald (1688-1744). He had given Pope great offence after his edition of Shakespeare appeared by drawing attention to its many errors and omissions in a volume called *Shakespeare Restored*, 1726. Theobald sometimes emended a passage by altering a single letter, or even a point of punctuation.

20 Of Hairs, or Straws, or Dirt, or Grubs, or Worms:
  The *Thing*, we know, is neither rich nor rare,
  Yet wonder how the Devil it got there.
      Are others angry? I excuse them too,
  Well may they rage, I give them *but* their Due.
25 Each Man's true Merit 'tis not hard to find;
  But each Man's secret Standard in his Mind,
  That casting Weight, Pride adds to Emptiness;
  This, who can *gratify*? For who can *guess*?
  The Wretch whom pilfer'd Pastorals renown,
30 Who turns a Persian Tale for half a Crown,
  Just writes to make his Barrenness appear,
  And strains, from hard bound Brains, six Lines a Year;
  In Sense still wanting, tho' he lives on Theft,
  Steals much, spends little, yet has nothing left:
35 Johnson, who now to Sense, now Nonsense leaning,
  Means not, but blunders round about a Meaning;
  And he, whose Fustian's so sublimely bad,
  It is not Poetry, but Prose run mad:
  Should modest Satire bid all these *translate*,
40 And own that nine such Poets make a Tate;

27 *casting Weight:* the weight that turns the scale.

29-30 *The Wretch . . . Crown:* Ambrose Philips, whose *Pastorals* owed a good deal to Theocritus, Virgil, and, above all, to Spenser. In 1709 he translated a volume of *Persian Tales* (from the French). According to Dr. Johnson, the payment of half-a-crown was for each "section", i.e. each tale. He added that this was liberal payment for those days, but "half-a-crown had a mean sound".

32 *hard bound Brains:* To call a writer "slow" was a recognised way of saying that he was dull. Pope has "slow Philips" in *Dunciad*, i, 238.

35 *Johnson:* Charles Johnson (1679-1748), dramatist, had sneered at *Three Hours after Marriage* (by Gay, Pope and Arbuthnot) in the prologue to *The Sultaness*, 1717. Pope, like other people, was particularly touchy about his failures.

38 *It is not . . . mad:* A note by Pope ascribes this verse to Dr. Abel Evans (1679-1737).

40 *Tate:* Nahum Tate (1652-1715), poet-laureate. According to Pope, he was "a cold writer of no *invention*, but sometimes translated tolerably" (*Dunciad*, i, 238).

How would they fume, and stamp, and roar, and chafe!
How would they swear, not Congreve's self were safe!
    Peace to all such! but were there one, whose Fires
Apollo kindled, and fair Fame inspires,
45 Blest with each Talent, and each Art to please,
And born to write, converse, and live with ease;
Should such a Man, too fond to rule alone,
Bear, like the Turk, no Brother near the Throne;
View him with scornful, yet with fearful eyes,
50 And hate for Arts that caus'd himself to rise;
Damn with faint Praise, assent with civil Leer,
And without sneering, teach the rest to sneer;
Wishing to wound, and yet afraid to strike,
Just hint a Fault, and hesitate Dislike;
55 Alike reserv'd to blame, or to commend,
A tim'rous Foe, and a suspicious Friend,
Dreading ev'n Fools, by Flatterers besieg'd,
And so obliging that he ne'er oblig'd:
Who, if two Wits on rival Themes contest,
60 Approves of each, but likes the worst the best;
Like Cato gives his *little Senate* Laws,
And sits attentive to his own Applause;

47 *too fond to rule:* i.e. too fond of ruling.

48 *Bear like the Turk, etc.:* In an otherwise laudatory notice of Pope's *Essay on Criticism* in *Spectator*, no. 253, Addison had reproached him for introducing some satirical touches on his contemporaries, and had cited some lines of Sir John Denham praising John Fletcher without dispraising his fellow writers:

> Nor needs thy juster Title the foul guilt
> Of Eastern Kings, who to secure their reign,
> Must have their Brothers, Sons, and Kindred slain.

Pope is here turning the quotation back on Addison.

51-2 *Damn . . . sneer:* In an account of Esther Johnson (Stella) written by Swift after her death, he notes that she much approved of a practice of Addison: ". . . when she saw any of the company very warm in a wrong opinion, she was more inclined to confirm them in it, than oppose them."

59-60 *Who, if two Wits . . . best:* See headnote to this poem.

61 *Cato:* alluding to Addison's celebrated tragedy of that name. His "little Senate" was the little circle of his admirers at Button's Coffee-house.

While Wits and Templars ev'ry Sentence raise,
And wonder with a foolish Face of Praise.
65 What Pity, Heav'n! if such a Man there be.
Who would not weep, if A[ddiso]n were he?

63 *ev'ry Sentence raise:* make every sententious remark sound better than it is.

THE LAMENTATION OF GLUMDALCLITCH, FOR THE LOSS OF GRILDRIG

A Pastoral

THIS is one of several poems written shortly after the publication of *Gulliver's Travels* in 1726. Glumdalclitch is the gigantic farmer's daughter ("not above forty foot high, being little for her age") who was so kind to Gulliver in Brobdingnag, and who gave him the name of Grildrig. The Queen of the Brobdingnagians had ordered a small box, about twelve feet square, to be made for Gulliver's convenience while travelling about the country, and the faithful Glumdalclitch accompanied him everywhere. One day, however, when the King and Queen had taken him on a visit to the south coast of the kingdom, Glumdalclitch became ill and Gulliver was left in the charge of a young page. This boy set the box down near the sea, and wandered off (so Gulliver conjectures) to look for birds' eggs among the rocks. While he was absent, a large bird of prey swooped down, and getting the ring of the box in its beak, soared away over the sea with the helpless Gulliver. The "Lamentation" describes the grief of Glumdalclitch when she discovers that her beloved Grildrig has disappeared. This poem cannot be ascribed with absolute certainty to Pope; it has also been claimed for Gay, or alternatively thought to be the joint work of both poets. Either could have written it; but the "Lamentation" shows the same imaginative awareness of the contrast between the tiny and the vast that Pope had already exploited so happily in his treatment of the sylphs in *The Rape of the Lock*. The text is that of *Miscellanies. The Fourth Volume*, 1742.

Soon as Glumdalclitch mist her pleasing Care,
She wept, she blubber'd, and she tore her Hair.
No British Miss sincerer Grief has known,
Her Squirrel missing, or her Sparrow flown.
5 She furl'd her Sampler, and hawl'd in her Thread,
And stuck her Needle into Grildrig's Bed;

Then spread her Hands, and with a Bounce let fall
Her Baby, like the Giant in Guild-hall.
In Peals of Thunder now she roars, and now
10 She gently whimpers like a lowing Cow.
Yet lovely in her Sorrow still appears:
Her Locks dishevell'd, and her Flood of Tears
Seem like the lofty Barn of some rich Swain,
When from the Thatch drips fast a Show'r of Rain.

15   In vain she search'd each Cranny of the House,
Each gaping Chink impervious to a Mouse.
"Was it for this (she cry'd) with daily Care
Within thy Reach I set the Vinegar?
And fill'd the Cruet with the Acid Tide,
20 While Pepper-Water-Worms thy Bait supply'd;
Where twin'd the Silver Eel around thy Hook,
And all the little Monsters of the Brook.
Sure in that Lake he dropt—My Grilly's drown'd"—
She dragg'd the Cruet, but no Grildrig found.

25   "Vain is thy Courage, Grilly, vain thy Boast;
But little Creatures enterprise the most.
Trembling, I've seen thee dare the Kitten's Paw;
Nay, mix with Children, as they play'd at Taw;
Nor fear the Marbles, as they bounding flew:
30 Marbles to them, but rolling Rocks to you.

      "Why did I trust thee with that giddy Youth?
Who from a Page can ever learn the Truth?
Vers'd in Court Tricks, that Money-loving Boy
To some Lord's Daughter sold the living Toy;

8 *Baby:* doll.   *the Giant in Guild-hall:* one of the two giant figures of
Gog and Magog in the Guildhall of London.

20 *Pepper-Water:* an infusion of black pepper used to examine animal-
culae under the microscope.

21 *Eel:* vinegar-eel.

26 *enterprise:* venture.

28 *Taw:* a game played with marbles.

35 Or rent him Limb from Limb in cruel Play,
   As Children tear the Wings of Flies away:
   From Place to Place o'er Brobdingnag I'll roam,
   And never will return, or bring thee home.
   But who hath Eyes to trace the passing Wind,
40 How then thy Fairy Footsteps can I find?
   Dost thou bewilder'd wander all alone,
   In the green Thicket of a Mossy Stone,
   Or tumbled from the Toadstool's slipp'ry Round,
   Perhaps all maim'd, lie grov'ling on the Ground?
45 Dost thou, inbosom'd in the lovely Rose,
   Or sunk within the Peach's Down, repose?
   Within the King-Cup if thy Limbs are spread,
   Or in the golden Cowslip's Velvet Head;
   O show me, Flora, 'midst those Sweets, the Flow'r
50 Where sleeps my Grildrig in his fragrant Bow'r!

     But ah! I fear thy little Fancy roves
   On little Females, and on little Loves;
   Thy Pigmy Children, and thy tiny Spouse,
   The Baby Play-things that adorn thy House,
55 Doors, Windows, Chimnies, and the spacious Rooms,
   Equal in Size to Cells of Honeycombs.
   Hast thou for these now ventur'd from the Shore,
   Thy Bark a Bean-shell, and a Straw thy Oar?
   Or in thy Box, now bounding on the Main?
60 Shall I ne'er bear thy self and House again?
   And shall I set thee on my Hand no more,
   To see thee leap the Lines, and traverse o'er
   My spacious Palm? Of Stature scarce a Span,
   Mimick the Actions of a real Man?
65 No more behold thee turn my Watches Key,
   As Seamen at a Capstern Anchors weigh?

38 *or bring:* i.e. or else I will bring.
49 *Flora:* the goddess of flowers and gardens.
63 *a Span:* the distance between Glumdalclitch's thumb and the tip of
her little finger when the hand is fully extended.
66 *Capstern:* capstan.

How wert thou wont to walk with cautious Tread,
A Dish of Tea like Milk-Pail on thy Head?
How chase the Mite that bore thy Cheese away,
70   And keep the rolling Maggot at a Bay?"

She said, but broken Accents stopt her Voice,
Soft as the Speaking Trumpet's mellow Noise:
She sobb'd a Storm, and wip'd her flowing Eyes,
Which seem'd like two broad Suns in misty Skies:
75   O squander not thy Grief, those Tears command
To weep upon our Cod in Newfound-land:
The plenteous Pickle shall preserve the Fish,
And Europe taste thy Sorrows in a Dish.

AN EPISTLE
TO
RICHARD BOYLE, EARL OF BURLINGTON

THIS poem, published in December 1731, is one of four Ethical Epistles
written between 1731 and 1735 which Pope's first editor, Warburton, was
later to call Moral Essays. Pope had at one time contemplated a *magnum
opus* in four books to be called "An Essay on Man"; this would have included the four epistles to which he actually gave that title, some parts of
the *Dunciad*, and the four ethical epistles already mentioned. These last
would have formed part of the fourth book which was to deal with private
ethics or practical morality. In the *Epistle to Bathurst*, which also deals with
the use of riches, Pope had contrasted the two extremes of avarice and
prodigality, and found virtue to lie in the happy medium. In the *Epistle to
Burlington* he is concerned with the misuse of riches, especially in architecture and gardening, by people with little or no taste or good sense. The
half-title of the first edition has the words "Of Taste", and in some later
editions this was altered to "Of False Taste". The main ideas in the poem
are set out in the following "Argument", which was added in 1735:

The vanity of expence in people of wealth and quality. The abuse of the
word Taste, v. 13. That the first principle and foundation in this as in
every thing else, is Good Sense, v. 40. The chief proof of it is to follow
Nature, even in works of mere luxury and elegance. Instanced in Architecture and Gardening, where all must be adapted to the genius and use
of the place, and the beauties not forced into it, but resulting from it,

v. 50. How men are disappointed in their most expensive undertakings, for want of this true foundation, without which nothing can please long, if at all; and the best examples and rules will but be perverted into something burdensome or ridiculous, vv. 65 to 92. A description of the false taste of magnificence; the first grand error of which is to imagine that greatness consists in the size and dimension, instead of the proportion and harmony of the whole, v. 97, and the second, either in joining together parts incoherent, or too minutely resembling, or in the repetition of the same too frequently, v. 105, etc. A word or two of false taste in books, in music, in painting, even in preaching and prayer, and lastly in entertainments, v. 133, etc. Yet Providence is justified in giving wealth to be squandered in this manner, since it is dispersed to the poor and laborious part of mankind, v. 169. What are the proper objects of magnificence, and a proper field for the expence of Great Men, v. 177, etc., and finally, the great and public works which become a Prince, v. 191, to the end.

> 'Tis strange, the Miser should his Cares employ,
> To gain those Riches he can ne'er enjoy:
> Is it less strange, the Prodigal should wast
> His wealth, to purchase what he ne'er can taste?
> 5 Not for himself he sees, or hears, or eats;
> Artists must chuse his Pictures, Music, Meats:
> He buys for Topham, Drawings and Designs,
> For Pembroke Statues, dirty Gods and Coins;
> Rare monkish Manuscripts for Hearne alone,
> 10 And Books for Mead, and Butterflies for Sloane.
> Think we all these are for himself? no more
> Than his fine Wife, alas! or finer Whore.

6 *Artists:* experts.

7 *Topham:* Richard Topham (d. 1735), who collected drawings, paintings and engravings.

8 *Pembroke:* Thomas Herbert, eighth Earl of Pembroke, another celebrated but undiscriminating collector.   *dirty:* because they had been dug up in Greece or Italy.

9 *Hearne:* Thomas Hearne, a learned Oxford scholar and editor of medieval chronicles.

10 *Mead:* Richard Mead, a wealthy physician who built up a valuable library of books.

10 *Sloane:* Sir Hans Sloane, also a physician, whose great collection of natural curiosities formed the nucleus of the British Museum.

> For what has Virro painted, built, and planted?
> Only to show, how many Tastes he wanted.
> 15 What brought Sir Visto's ill got wealth to waste?
> Some Dæmon whisper'd, 'Visto! have a Taste.'
> Heav'n visits with a Taste the wealthy fool,
> And needs no Rod but Ripley with a Rule.
> See! sportive fate, to punish aukward pride,
> 20 Bids Bubo build, and sends him such a Guide:
> A standing sermon, at each year's expence,
> That never Coxcomb reach'd Magnificence!
> You show us, Rome was glorious, not profuse,
> And pompous buildings once were things of Use.
> 25 Yet shall (my Lord) your just, your noble rules
> Fill half the land with Imitating Fools;
> Who random drawings from your sheets shall take,
> And of one beauty many blunders make;
> Load some vain Church with old Theatric state,
> 30 Turn Arcs of triumph to a Garden-gate;
> Reverse your Ornaments, and hang them all
> On some patch'd dog-hole ek'd with ends of wall,
> Then clap four slices of Pilaster on't,
> That, lac'd with bits of rustic, makes a Front.

13, 15 *Virro . . . Sir Visto:* examples of "the wealthy fool" of l. 17.

18 *no Rod:* i.e. no rod to punish (but with a pun on the builder's measuring-rod).   *Ripley:* Thomas Ripley (d. 1758). "This man was a carpenter, employ'd by a first Minister, who rais'd him to an Architect, without any genius in the art; and after some wretched proofs of his insufficiency in public Buildings, made him Comptroller of the Board of Works." [Pope.]

20 *Bubo:* George Bubb Dodington, a wealthy country gentleman and politician, whose house in Dorset was enlarged at great expense by Vanbrugh.

23-4 *You show us, etc.:* "The Earl of Burlington was then publishing the Designs of Inigo Jones, and the Antiquities of Rome by Palladio." [Pope.] *The Designs of Inigo Jones* appeared in 1727, and the *Fabriche antiche . . .* of Andrea Palladio in 1730.

32 *dog-hole:* "a mean habitation" (Johnson's *Dictionary*).

33 *Pilaster:* a pillar built into a wall.

34 *rustic:* an architectural term describing a surface artificially roughened or left rough-hewn.

35 Or call the winds thro' long Arcades to roar,
    Proud to catch cold at a Venetian door;
    Conscious they act a true Palladian part,
    And if they starve, they starve by rules of art.
        Oft have you hinted to your brother Peer,
40 A certain truth, which many buy too dear:
    Something there is more needful than Expence,
    And something previous ev'n to Taste—'tis Sense:
    Good Sense, which only is the gift of Heav'n,
    And tho' no science, fairly worth the sev'n:
45 A Light, which in yourself you must perceive;
    Jones and Le Nôtre have it not to give.
        To build, to plant, whatever you intend,
    To rear the Column, or the Arch to bend,
    To swell the Terras, or to sink the Grot;
50 In all, let Nature never be forgot.
    But treat the Goddess like a modest fair,
    Nor over-dress, nor leave her wholly bare;
    Let not each beauty ev'ry where be spy'd,
    Where half the skill is decently to hide.
55 He gains all points, who pleasingly confounds,
    Surprizes, varies, and conceals the Bounds.
        Consult the Genius of the Place in all;
    That tells the Waters or to rise, or fall,
    Or helps th' ambitious Hill the heav'n to scale,
60 Or scoops in circling theatres the Vale,
    Calls in the Country, catches opening glades,
    Joins willing woods, and varies shades from shades,

---

36 *Venetian door:* "A Door or Window, so called, from being much practised at Venice, by Palladio and others." [Pope.]

38 *starve:* die of cold.

44 *the sev'n:* i.e. the seven liberal arts and sciences.

46 *Jones . . . Le Nôtre:* For Inigo Jones (1573-1652), cf. ll. 23-4. André le Nôtre (1613-1700) laid out the gardens at Versailles and Fontainebleau.

47-98 Pope now deals with taste in landscape-gardening.

55 *He gains all points:* Cf. Horace, *Ars Poetica*, l. 343: *omne tulit punctum.*

56 *conceals the Bounds:* This was frequently done by the use of a "ha-ha", i.e. a sunk fence.

Now breaks or now directs th' intending Lines;
Paints as you plant, and, as you work, designs.

65   Still follow Sense, of ev'ry Art the Soul,
Parts answ'ring parts shall slide into a whole,
Spontaneous beauties all around advance,
Start ev'n from Difficulty, strike from Chance;
Nature shall join you, Time shall make it grow

70   A Work to wonder at—perhaps a Stow.
     Without it, proud Versailles! thy glory falls;
And Nero's Terraces desert their walls:
The vast Parterres a thousand hands shall make,
Lo! Cobham comes, and floats them with a Lake:

75   Or cut wide views thro' Mountains to the Plain,
You'll wish your hill or shelter'd seat again.
Ev'n in an ornament its place remark,
Nor in an Hermitage set Dr. Clarke.
     Behold Villario's ten-years toil compleat;

80   His Quincunx darkens, his Espaliers meet,
The Wood supports the Plain, the parts unite,
And strength of Shade contends with strength of Light;
A waving Glow his bloomy beds display,
Blushing in bright diversities of day,

63 *intending:* having a purpose or design.

68 *strike:* take root.

70 *Stow:* the seat of Richard Temple, Viscount Cobham, in Buckinghamshire. For its lake, see l. 74.

71 *it:* i.e. good sense.

72 *Nero's Terraces:* in his palace called the Golden House.

73 *Parterres:* level spaces filled with flower-beds.

74 *floats:* inundates.

78 *Hermitage . . . Dr. Clarke:* In the Hermitage, an ornamental construction in Richmond Park, Queen Caroline had set up various busts, including one of Dr. Samuel Clarke the philosopher.

79 *Villario:* possibly the Earl of Castlemaine, the owner of a fine mansion in Essex.

80 *Quincunx:* a group of trees in the shape of a square or rectangle, with a fifth tree planted in the middle.

85 With silver-quiv'ring rills mæander'd o'er—
Enjoy them, you! Villario can no more;
Tir'd of the scene Parterres and Fountains yield,
He finds at last he better likes a Field.
    Thro' his young Woods how pleas'd Sabinus stray'd,
90 Or sat delighted in the thick'ning shade
With annual joy the red'ning shoots to greet,
Or see the stretching branches long to meet!
His Son's fine Taste an op'ner Vista loves,
Foe to the Dryads of his Father's groves,
95 One boundless Green, or flourish'd Carpet views,
With all the mournful family of Yews;
The thriving plants ignoble broomsticks made,
Now sweep those Alleys they were born to shade.
    At Timon's Villa let us pass a day,
100 Where all cry out, "What sums are thrown away!"
So proud, so grand, of that stupendous air,
Soft and Agreeable come never there.
Greatness, with Timon, dwells in such a draught
As brings all Brobdignag before your thought.
105 To compass this, his building is a Town,
His pond an Ocean, his parterre a Down:
Who but must laugh, the Master when he sees,
A puny insect, shiv'ring at a breeze!
Lo, what huge heaps of littleness around!
110 The whole, a labour'd Quarry above ground.
Two Cupids squirt before: a Lake behind
Improves the keeness of the Northern wind.
His Gardens next your admiration call,
On ev'ry side you look, behold the Wall!
115 No pleasing Intricacies intervene,

98 *Timon's Villa:* It was generally believed that Timon was intended for James Brydges, Duke of Chandos, whose country house (Cannons) was situated near Edgware; but Pope denied that he was meant. Both the character of Timon and the villa may be composite pictures.
  103 *in such a draught:* in such a (huge) design.
  110 *labour'd:* (1) built with great labour; (2) over-elaborate.
  113 *admiration:* (1) wonder; (2) (sarcastically) approbation.

No artful wildness to perplex the scene;
Grove nods at grove, each Alley has a brother,
And half the platform just reflects the other.
The suff'ring eye inverted Nature sees,
120 Trees cut to Statues, Statues thick as trees,
With here a Fountain, never to be play'd,
And there a Summer-house, that knows no shade;
Here Amphitrite sails thro' myrtle bow'rs;
There Gladiators fight, or die, in flow'rs;
125 Un-water'd see the drooping sea-horse mourn,
And swallows roost in Nilus' dusty Urn.
    My Lord advances with majestic mien,
Smit with the mighty pleasure, to be seen:
But soft—by regular approach—not yet—
130 First thro' the length of yon hot Terrace sweat,
And when up ten steep slopes you've dragg'd your thighs,
Just at his Study-door he'll bless your eyes.
    His Study! with what Authors is it stor'd?
In Books, not Authors, curious is my Lord;
135 To all their dated Backs he turns you round,
These Aldus printed, those Du Sueil has bound.
Lo some are Vellom, and the rest as good
For all his Lordship knows, but they are Wood.
For Locke or Milton 'tis in vain to look,
140 These shelves admit not any modern book.
    And now the Chapel's silver bell you hear,
That summons you to all the Pride of Pray'r:

116 *perplex:* make more intricate.

118 *platform:* a terrace on the top of a wall.

123 *Amphitrite:* daughter of Oceanus and wife of Neptune. The Amphitrite and the gladiators of l. 124 are examples of statues placed in a wrong setting.

126 *Urn:* the urn which river-gods are shown as carrying in classical art. The sea-horse is "unwater'd" and the urn of Nilus is "dusty" because these figures are placed in a dried-up fountain.

136 *Aldus:* Aldo Manutio, the famous Italian printer of the Renaissance. *Du Sueil:* a celebrated Parisian bookbinder of Pope's day.

138 *Wood:* i.e. imitations of the backs of books painted on wood.

Light quirks of Musick, broken and uneven,
Make the soul dance upon a Jig to Heaven.
145 On painted Cielings you devoutly stare,
Where sprawl the Saints of Verrio or Laguerre,
On gilded clouds in fair expansion lie,
And bring all Paradise before your eye.
To rest, the Cushion and soft Dean invite,
150 Who never mentions Hell to ears polite.
    But hark! the chiming Clocks to dinner call;
A hundred footsteps scrape the marble Hall:
The rich Buffet well-colour'd Serpents grace,
And gaping Tritons spew to wash your face.
155 Is this a dinner? this a Genial room?
No, 'tis a Temple, and a Hecatomb.
A solemn Sacrifice, perform'd in state,
You drink by measure, and to minutes eat.
So quick retires each flying course, you'd swear
160 Sancho's dread Doctor and his Wand were there.
Between each Act the trembling salvers ring,
From soup to sweet-wine, and God bless the King.
In plenty starving, tantaliz'd in state,
And complaisantly help'd to all I hate,
165 Treated, caress'd, and tir'd, I take my leave,
Sick of his civil Pride from Morn to Eve;

143 *Light quirks of Music:* "The false Taste in Music, improper to the subjects, as of light airs in Churches, often practised by the organists, etc." [Pope.]

146 *the Saints of Verrio or Laguerre:* A note by Pope makes it clear that he was objecting to "naked figures in Churches, etc." Antonio Verrio (1639-1726) and Louis Laguerre (1663-1721) had both painted a number of ceilings, altar-pieces, etc. for English houses and churches.

150 *Who never mentions Hell . . . :* "This is a fact; a reverend Dean preaching at Court, threatened the sinner with punishment in 'a place which he thought it not decent to name in so polite an assembly'." [Pope.]

153 *Buffet:* sideboard.

154 *gaping Tritons:* They are ejecting water into a fountain.

156 *Hecatomb:* (literally) a public sacrifice of a hundred oxen.

160 *Sancho's dread Doctor:* See *Don Quixote*, ch. xlvii.

165 *Treated:* entertained with food and drink.

I curse such lavish cost, and little skill,
And swear no Day was ever past so ill.
    Yet hence the Poor are cloath'd, the Hungry fed;
170 Health to himself, and to his Infants bread
The Lab'rer bears: What his hard Heart denies,
His charitable Vanity supplies.
    Another age shall see the golden Ear
Imbrown the Slope, and nod on the Parterre,
175 Deep Harvests bury all his pride has plann'd,
And laughing Ceres re-assume the land.
    Who then shall grace, or who improve the Soil?
Who plants like Bathurst, or who builds like Boyle.
'Tis Use alone that sanctifies Expence,
180 And Splendor borrows all her rays from Sense.
    His Father's Acres who enjoys in peace,
Or makes his Neighbours glad, if he encrease;
Whose chearful Tenants bless their yearly toil,
Yet to their Lord owe more than to the soil;
185 Whose ample Lawns are not asham'd to feed
The milky heifer and deserving steed;
Whose rising Forests, not for pride or show,
But future Buildings, future Navies grow:
Let his plantations stretch from down to down,
190 First shade a Country, and then raise a Town.
    You too proceed! make falling Arts your care,
Erect new wonders, and the old repair,

169 ff. The doctrine that "private vices are public benefits" had been argued by Pope's contemporary, Bernard Mandeville, in *The Fable of the Bees*.

    171 *his:* i.e. Timon's.

    176 *Ceres:* the goddess of harvests.

    178 *Bathurst:* Allen, Lord Bathurst, who was a keen landscape-gardener. *Boyle:* the Earl of Burlington to whom the epistle is addressed.

    179 *Use:* utility, profit.

    182 *encrease:* grow richer.

    185 *Lawns:* open stretches of grassy land. Cf. *Winter*, p. 172, l. 86.

    190 *Country:* a rural district.

    191 *You:* i.e. Burlington.

Jones and Palladio to themselves restore,
And be whate'er Vitruvius was before:
195 Till Kings call forth th' Idea's of your mind,
Proud to accomplish what such hands design'd,
Bid Harbors open, public Ways extend,
Bid Temples, worthier of the God, ascend;
Bid the broad Arch the dang'rous Flood contain,
200 The Mole projected break the roaring Main;
Back to his bounds their subject Sea command,
And roll obedient Rivers thro' the Land;
These Honours, Peace to happy Britain brings,
These are Imperial Works, and worthy Kings.

194 *Vitruvius:* M. Vitruvius Pollio, a celebrated architect of the time of the Emperor Augustus.

195-204 "The poet after having touched upon the proper objects of Magnificence and Expence, in the private works of great men, comes to those great and public works which become a Prince." [Pope.] He is referring to new harbours and turnpike roads (197), new churches (198), Westminster Bridge (199), and the repairing of the breach which had been made at Dagenham in Essex by a great storm in 1707, when a large tract of country in the Thames estuary had been flooded (200-202).

AN ODE FOR THE NEW YEAR.
WRITTEN BY COLLEY CIBBER, ESQ.
POET LAUREAT

THIS satirical "ode" in ballad measure cannot be ascribed with absolute certainty to Pope, but a strong case for Pope's authorship was made out by Norman Ault in his *New Light on Pope*, and it would be difficult to find a better candidate for this brilliant skit. Colley Cibber had been appointed poet-laureate in 1730, and in accordance with tradition had to produce an annual Ode for the New Year and another for the King's birthday. His offerings were among the worst of their kind, and excited much ribald comment. This satirical piece first appeared in an undated broadside which Mr. Ault assigned to the year 1733. In support of this dating he pointed to ll. 23-4 which, he argued, must refer to the War of the Polish Succession: George II wished England to intervene, but his first minister, Sir Robert Walpole, insisted on the country remaining neutral. Similarly, the wish that Frederick, Prince of Wales, may have some "Money in his Purse" (40) must refer to the political agitation, which began in 1733, to increase his allowance; and "All marry *gratis*, Boy and Miss" (45) appears to allude to the parsimonious entertainment given by George II to the Prince of Orange when he came to England in 1733 to meet his future bride, the Princess Royal. It is not surprising that the "ode" was published anonymously: mockery of Cibber was harmless enough, but such dangerous ridicule of the royal family might have had serious consequences. The text is that of the undated broadside, but one or two blanks (e.g. K**g, F**l) have been filled in.

> God prosper long our gracious King,
>   Now sitting on the Throne,
> Who leads this Nation in a *String*,
>   And governs all but *One*.
>
> 5   This is the Day when, right or wrong,
>   I Colley Bays, Esquire,
> Must, for my Sack, indite a Song,
>   And thrum my *Venal Lyre*.
>
> Not he, who rul'd great Judah's Realm,
> 10   Ycleped Solomon,
> Was wiser than ours at the Helm,
>   Or had a *wiser Son*.
>
> He rak'd up Wealth to glut his Fill,
>   In Drinking, Whores, and Houses,
> 15   Which wiser George can save, to fill
>   His Pocket, and his Spouse's.
>
> His Head with Wisdom deep is fraught,
>   His Breast with Courage glows,
> Alas! how mournful is the Thought,
> 20   He ever shou'd want Foes.

3 *leads . . . in a String:* has the nation under control, is able to do what he likes with it. (String = leading-string).

4 *One:* The "one" was Queen Caroline, who was much more intelligent than the King, and, with the help of Sir Robert Walpole (the "Bob" of l. 36), "managed" him.

7 *Sack:* The Poet Laureate received a butt of canary wine (often referred to as "sack") as one of his perquisites.

For at his Heart he loves a Drum,
  As Children love a Rattle,
If not in Field, in Drawing-Room,
  He daily sounds to Battle.

25 The Queen I also pray God save,
  His Consort, plump, and dear,
Who, just as he is *Wise* and *Brave*,
  Is *Pious* and *Sincere*.

She's courteous, good, and charms all Folks,
30 Loves one as well as t'other,
Of Arian and of Orthodox,
  Alike the Nursing Mother.

Oh! may she always meet Success
  In ev'ry Scheme and Job,
35 And still continue to caress
  That honest Statesman Bob.

God send the Prince, that Babe of Grace,
  A little Whore and Horse,
A little Meaning in his Face,
40 And Money in his Purse.

Heav'n spread o'er all his Family
  That broad *Illustrious Glare*,
Which shines so flat in ev'ry Eye,
  And makes 'em all *so stare*.

28 *Pious:* The Queen's orthodoxy was suspect; she was certainly very tolerant in her religious views.

31 *Arian:* The Arians denied the divinity of Christ.

42 *Illustrious Glare:* a hereditary feature of the Hanoverian royal line. In *The Dunciad* of 1728 (i, 97-8) the goddess Dulness "saw with joy the line immortal run,/Each sire imprest and *glaring* in his son"—a barbed allusion to the recent accession of George II. In the same poem one of the dunces is said to have "pert *flat* eyes" (ii, 39).

45   All marry *gratis*, Boy and Miss,
      All still increase their Store,
  As in Beginning was, now is,
      And shall be evermore.

  But oh! ev'n Kings must die of Course,
50   And to their Heirs be Civil;
  We Poets too, on winged Horse,
      Must soon ride to the Devil.

  Then since I have a Son, like You,
      May he Parnassus rule;
55   So shall the Crown, and Laurel too,
      Descend from Fool to Fool.

53 *a Son:* Cibber's eldest son, Theophilus, was, like his father, an actor and playwright. His character was contemptible.

THE FIRST ODE OF THE FOURTH BOOK OF HORACE: TO VENUS

THIS imitation of Horace was published in 1737. Horace wrote his ode when he was approaching his fiftieth birthday, and Pope, who was born in May 1688, was reaching the same age in 1737. His version of Horace's ode should be compared with that of Nicholas Rowe on p. 34. Rowe's poem is the more romantic, and the movement of his verse is more lyrical: Pope's rendering is more controlled, and no doubt nearer in tone and intention to Horace.

  Again? new Tumults in my Breast?
  Ah spare me, Venus! let me, let me rest!
     I am not now, alas! the man
  As in the gentle Reign of My Queen Anne.
5   Ah sound no more thy soft alarms,
  Nor circle sober fifty with thy Charms.

4 *in the gentle Reign of My Queen Anne:* Pope's rendering of Horace's *bonae sub regno Cynarae* ("under the sway of kindly Cynara"—Horace's mistress).

Mother too fierce of dear Desires!
Turn, turn to willing Hearts your wanton fires.
    To *Number five* direct your Doves,
10 There spread round Murray all your blooming Loves;
    Noble and young, who strikes the heart
With every sprightly, every decent part;
    Equal, the injur'd to defend,
To charm the Mistress, or to fix the Friend.
15   He, with a hundred Arts refin'd,
Shall stretch thy Conquests over half the kind:
    To him each Rival shall submit,
Make but his riches equal to his Wit.
    Then shall thy Form the Marble grace,
20 (Thy Græcian Form) and Chloe lend the Face:
    His House, embosom'd in the Grove,
Sacred to social Life and social Love,
    Shall glitter o'er the pendent green,
Where Thames reflects the visionary Scene.
25   Thither, the silver-sounding Lyres
Shall call the smiling Loves, and young Desires;
    There, every Grace and Muse shall throng,
Exalt the Dance, or animate the Song;
    There, Youths and Nymphs, in consort gay,
30 Shall hail the rising, close the parting day.
    With me, alas! those joys are o'er;
For me, the vernal Garlands bloom no more.
    Adieu! fond hope of mutual fire,
The still-believing, still-renew'd desire;
35   Adieu! the heart-expanding bowl,
And all the kind Deceivers of the soul!

10 *Murray:* William Murray (1705-93), a rising young lawyer, living at
this time at No. 5 King's Bench Walk. Pope frequently referred to his
eloquence and charm. He eventually became Lord Chief Justice and Earl of
Mansfield.

14 *fix:* attach firmly.   16 *the kind:* the human race.

21-4 *His House . . . Scene:* Murray partially fulfilled this prophecy in
later life by building for himself the magnificent mansion which still stands
in Ken Wood.

> —But why? ah tell me, ah too dear!
>> Steals down my cheek th' involuntary Tear?
>> Why words so flowing, thoughts so free,
> 40   Stop, or turn nonsense at one glance of Thee?
>> Thee, drest in Fancy's airy beam,
>> Absent I follow thro' th' extended Dream,
>> Now, now I seize, I clasp thy charms,
>> And now you burst (ah cruel!) from my arms,
> 45   And swiftly shoot along the Mall,
>> Or softly glide by the Canal,
>> Now shown by Cynthia's silver Ray,
>> And now, on rolling Waters snatch'd away.

46 *the Canal:* the ponds in St. James's Park which had been joined into a continuous stretch of water early in the reign of Charles II.

CLOE: A CHARACTER

SOME at least of Pope's Epistles appear to have been composed of passages written at various times and later dovetailed together. In this way the Character of Addison eventually became part of the *Epistle to Dr. Arbuthnot*, and this Character of Cloe, first published in 1739, was included just before Pope's death in *Epistles to Several Persons* (1744), where it appeared as lines 157-180 of the Epistle to a Lady, "Of the Characters of Women". Cloe was generally thought in the eighteenth century to be based on Henrietta Howard, later Countess of Suffolk, a Woman of the Bedchamber to Queen Caroline and one of the mistresses of her husband, George II. (Cf. "Verses on the Death of Dr. Swift", p. 58, l. 179.)

> "Yet Cloe sure was form'd without a spot"—
> Nature in her then err'd not, but forgot.
> "With ev'ry pleasing, ev'ry prudent part,
> Say, what can Cloe want?"—She wants a Heart.
> 5 She speaks, behaves, and acts just as she ought;
> But never, never, reach'd one gen'rous Thought.
> Virtue she finds too painful an endeavour,
> Content to dwell in Decencies for ever.
> So very reasonable, so unmov'd,
> 10 As never yet to love, or to be lov'd.

She, while her Lover pants upon her breast,
Can mark the figures on an Indian chest;
And when she sees her Friend in deep despair,
Observes how much a Chintz exceeds Mohair.
15 Forbid it, Heav'n, a Favour or a Debt
She e'er should cancel—but she may forget.
Safe is your Secret still in Cloe's ear;
But none of Cloe's shall you ever hear.
Of all her Dears she never slander'd one,
20 But cares not if a thousand are undone.
Would Cloe know if you're alive or dead?
She bids her Footman put it in her head.
Cloe is prudent—Would you too be wise?
Then never break your heart when Cloe dies.

John Gay

TRIVIA;
OR, THE ART OF WALKING THE STREETS OF LONDON

Quo te Moeri pedes? An, quo via ducit, in Urbem? ★

ONE of the Latin poems most admired by eighteenth-century readers was Virgil's *Georgics*, the work in which he described the life of husbandmen, the cultivation of the land and the rearing of livestock. Several English poets wrote modern georgic poems, including Gay, whose *Rural Sports* was published in 1713. His *Trivia*† appeared three years later, and if we stretch the term a little, this poem in three books may be described as an urban georgic. In dealing with the art of walking the streets of London, Gay touches upon many of the characteristic occupations and activities and sights of a great city, and upon the daily life of its people. Like so much of

★ The motto ("Whither afoot, Moeris? Is it, as the way leads, to town?") is from Virgil, *Eclogue* ix, 1.

† *Trivia*: The title of Gay's poem comes from the goddess Diana, who was surnamed "Trivia" because she presided over all places where three roads met.

his poetry *Trivia* is written with an air of gentle mockery (the joke begins with the sedentary Gay walking at all), and the language has often that sort of elevation by which humble themes were "raised" and given the dignity then thought necessary for this kind of poetry. Book I deals with the "implements" (i.e. the right equipment) for walking the streets, and with the signs of the weather; and the general theme of Book III is "Of walking the streets by night". The text of Book II given here is, with some modifications of punctuation, that of the "third edition" of 1730, but the side-headings, which Gay later dropped, are inserted from the first edition of 1716. The episode of Cloacina (ll. 99-220) first appeared in the edition of 1720.

BOOK II

Thus far the Muse has trac'd in useful lays,
The proper implements for wintry ways;
Has taught the walker, with judicious eyes,
To read the various warnings of the skies.
5 Now venture, Muse, from home, to range the town,
And for the publique safety risque thy own.

The Morning.   For ease and for dispatch the morning's best;
No tides of passengers the street molest.
You'll see a draggled damsel, here and there,
10 From Billingsgate her fishy traffick bear;
On doors the sallow milk-maid chalks her gains;
Ah! how unlike the milk-maid of the plains!
Before proud gates attending asses bray,
Or arrogate with solemn pace the way;
15 These grave physicians with their milky cheer
The love-sick maid and dwindling beau repair;
Here rows of drummers stand in martial file,
And with their vellom thunder shake the pile,
To greet the new-made bride. Are sounds like these
20 The proper prelude to a state of peace?

2 *implements:* equipment. In Book I Gay had been discoursing on overcoats, canes, umbrellas, shoes, etc.

10 *Billingsgate:* the famous fish-market, a little below London Bridge. *traffick:* merchandise.

13 *asses:* asses' milk was in great demand for invalids. The ass was brought to the door and milked there.

17 *drummers:* Serenading of the newly-wed by drummers was a regular eighteenth-century custom.

Now industry awakes her busie sons,
Full charg'd with news the breathless hawker runs;
Shops open, coaches roll, carts shake the ground,
And all the streets with passing cries resound.

What Trades prejudicial to Walkers.

If cloath'd in black you tread the busy town,
Or if distinguish'd by the rev'rend gown,
Three trades avoid; oft in the mingling press
The barber's apron soils the sable dress;
Shun the perfumer's touch with cautious eye,
30 Nor let the baker's step advance too nigh.
Ye walkers too that youthful colours wear,
Three sullying trades avoid with equal care;
The little chimney-sweeper skulks along,
And marks with sooty stains the heedless throng;
35 When small-coal murmurs in the hoarser throat,
From smutty dangers guard thy threaten'd coat:
The dust-man's cart offends thy cloaths and eyes,
When through the street a cloud of ashes flies;
But whether black or lighter dyes are worn,
40 The chandler's-basket, on his shoulder born,
With tallow spots thy coat; resign the way,
To shun the surly butcher's greasy tray,
Butchers, whose hands are dy'd with blood's foul stain,
And always foremost in the hangman's train.

To whom to give the Wall.

Let due civilities be strictly paid.
The wall surrender to the hooded maid;
Nor let thy sturdy elbow's hasty rage
Jostle the feeble steps of trembling age:

---

22 *hawker:* newspaper-seller.

33 *little chimney-sweeper:* In view of the adjective it is clear that Gay is thinking of the little boys who were sent up inside chimneys to clean them.

35 *small-coal:* household coal (sometimes charcoal).

40 *chandler's:* The tallow-chandler made or sold candles.

46 *The wall:* "Giving the wall", i.e. allowing someone to pass on the inside, was an important concession in the narrow, dirty, and dangerous London streets.

And when the porter bends beneath his load,
50 And pants for breath; clear thou the crouded road.
But, above all, the groping blind direct,
And from the pressing throng the lame protect.
You'll sometimes meet a fop, of nicest tread,
Whose mantling peruke veils his empty head,
55 At ev'ry step he dreads the wall to lose,
And risques, to save a coach, his red-heel'd shoes;
Him, like the miller, pass with caution by,
Lest from his shoulder clouds of powder fly.

To whom to refuse the Wall.

But when the bully, with assuming pace,
Cocks his broad hat, edg'd round with tarnish'd lace,
Yield not the way; defie his strutting pride,
And thrust him to the muddy kennel's side;
He never turns again, nor dares oppose,
But mutters coward curses as he goes.

Of whom to enquire the Way.

If drawn by bus'ness to a street unknown,
Let the sworn porter point thee through the town;
Be sure observe the signs, for signs remain,
Like faithful land-marks to the walking train.
Seek not from prentices to learn the way,
70 Those fabling boys will turn thy steps astray;
Ask the grave tradesman to direct thee right,
He ne'er deceives, but when he profits by't.
Where famed St. Giles's ancient limits spread,
An inrail'd column rears its lofty head,

54 *mantling:* enveloping, concealing.   *peruke:* wig.

56 *red-heel'd shoes:* These were fashionable in the reign of Queen Anne and for some years later.

58 *powder:* i.e. from the fop's wig.

60 *Cocks his . . . hat:* a gesture of defiance.

62 *kennel's side:* The kennel was an open drain, often running down the middle of a street. Cf. "A Description of the Morning", p. 49, l. 10.

66 *sworn:* licensed.

67 *signs:* i.e. shop-signs, etc., which were large and numerous.

74 *column:* Seven Dials, in the parish of St. Giles-in-the-Fields, took its name from a column on top of which were seven sundials marking the points at which seven streets met.

75 Here to sev'n streets sev'n dials count the day,
    And from each other catch the circling ray.
    Here oft the peasant, with enquiring face,
    Bewilder'd, trudges on from place to place;
    He dwells on ev'ry sign with stupid gaze,
80 Enters the narrow alley's doubtful maze,
    Tries ev'ry winding court and street in vain,
    And doubles o'er his weary steps again.
    Thus hardy Theseus, with intrepid feet,
    Travers'd the dang'rous labyrinth of Crete;
85 But still the wandring passes forc'd his stay,
    Till Ariadne's clue unwinds the way.
    But do not thou, like that bold chief, confide
    Thy ventrous footsteps to a female guide;
    She'll lead thee with delusive smiles along,
90 Dive in thy fob, and drop thee in the throng.

Useful Precepts.

         When waggish boys the stunted beesom ply
    To rid the slabby pavement; pass not by
    E'er thou hast held their hands; some heedless flirt
    Will over-spread thy calves with spatt'ring dirt.
95 Where porters hogsheads roll from carts aslope,
    Or brewers down steep cellars stretch the rope,
    Where counted billets are by carmen tost;
    Stay thy rash step, and walk without the post.
         What though the gath'ring mire thy feet besmear,
100 The voice of industry is always near.

---

83 *Theseus:* The son of a King of Athens, he slew the Minotaur, a monster which King Minos of Crete had confined in a labyrinth. Ariadne, the daughter of Minos, who had fallen in love with Theseus, gave him a clue of thread by means of which he was able to extricate himself from the labyrinth.

90 *fob:* a pocket in the waistband of the breeches.

91-4 One of several reminiscences of Swift's "Description of the Morning". See p. 49, ll. 9-10.

92 *slabby:* muddy, slushy.

93 *flirt:* flick of the broom. Cf. Swift, "A City Shower", p. 50, l. 20.

97 *billets:* firewood.

98 *without the post:* outside the post, i.e. on the street. Posts were used to mark the boundary line between street and pavement. Cf. l. 228.

Hark! the boy calls thee to his destin'd stand,
And the shoe shines beneath his oily hand.
Here let the Muse, fatigu'd amid the throng,
Adorn her precepts with digressive song;
105 Of shirtless youths the secret rise to trace,
And show the parent of the sable race.

   Like mortal man, great Jove (grown fond of change)
Of old was wont this nether world to range
To seek amours; the vice the monarch lov'd
110 Soon through the wide etherial court improv'd,
And ev'n the proudest Goddess now and then
Would lodge a night among the sons of men;
To vulgar Deitys descends the fashion,
Each, like her betters, had her earthly passion.
115 Then Cloacina (Goddess of the tide
Whose sable streams beneath the city glide)
Indulg'd the modish flame; the town she rov'd,
A mortal scavenger she saw, she lov'd;
The muddy spots that dry'd upon his face,
120 Like female patches, heighten'd ev'ry grace:
She gaz'd; she sigh'd. For love can beauties spy
In what seems faults to every common eye.

   Now had the watchman walk'd his second round;
When Cloacina hears the rumbling sound
125 Of her brown lover's cart, for well she knows
That pleasing thunder: swift the Goddess rose,
And through the streets pursu'd the distant noise,
Her bosom panting with expected joys.
With the night-wandring harlot's airs she past,
130 Brush'd near his side, and wanton glances cast;

101 *destin'd:* appointed.   **110** *improv'd:* increased.
115 *Cloacina:* "Cloacina was a Goddess whose image Tatius (a King of the Sabines) found in the common-shore, and not knowing what Goddess it was, he called it Cloacina from the place in which it was found, and paid it divine honours" [Gay]. *Cloaca* is the Latin word for sewer.
120 *patches:* small pieces of black silk worn on the face by women of fashion.

In the black form of cinder-wench she came,
When love, the hour, the place had banish'd shame;
To the dark alley, arm in arm they move:
O may no link-boy interrupt their love!
135 When the pale moon had nine times fill'd her
   space,
The pregnant Goddess (cautious of disgrace)
Descends to earth; but sought no midwife's aid,
Nor midst her anguish to Lucina pray'd;
No cheerful gossip wish'd the mother joy,
140 Alone, beneath a bulk, she dropt the boy.
  The child through various risques in years im-
   prov'd,
At first a beggar's brat, compassion mov'd;
His infant tongue soon learnt the canting art,
Knew all the pray'rs and whines to touch the heart.
145 Oh happy unown'd youths, your limbs can bear
The scorching dog-star, and the winter's air,
While the rich infant, nurs'd with care and pain,
Thirsts with each heat, and coughs with ev'ry rain!
  The Goddess long had mark'd the child's distress,
150 And long had sought his suff'rings to redress;
She prays the Gods to take the fondling's part,
To teach his hands some beneficial art
Practis'd in streets: the Gods her suit allow'd,
And made him useful to the walking croud,
155 To cleanse the miry feet, and o'er the shoe
With nimble skill the glossy black renew.

131 *cinder-wench:* "a female whose occupation it is to rake cinders from among ashes" (O.E.D.).

134 *link-boy:* a boy carrying a torch (link) to light pedestrians through the streets.

138 *Lucina:* the goddess to whom women prayed in childbirth.

139 *gossip:* female friend, more especially one invited to be present at a birth.

140 *bulk:* a shop-stall projecting from the front of the shop.

143 *canting art:* the lingo used by beggars.

146 *dog-star:* Sirius. Cf. Addison, "The Bowling-Green", p. 32, l. 81*n.*

Each Power contributes to relieve the poor:
With the strong bristles of the mighty boar
Diana forms his brush; the God of day
160 A tripod gives, amid the crouded way
To raise the dirty foot, and ease his toil;
Kind Neptune fills his vase with fetid oil
Prest from th' enormous whale; The God of fire,
From whose dominions smoaky clouds aspire,
165 Among these gen'rous presents joins his part,
And aids with soot the new japanning art:
Pleas'd she receives the gifts; she downward glides,
Lights in Fleet-ditch, and shoots beneath the tides.
   Now dawns the morn, the sturdy lad awakes,
170 Leaps from his stall, his tangled hair he shakes,
Then leaning o'er the rails, he musing stood,
And view'd below the black canal of mud,
Where common-shores a lulling murmur keep,
Whose torrents rush from Holborn's fatal steep:
175 Pensive through idleness, tears flow'd apace,
Which eas'd his loaded heart, and wash'd his face;
At length he sighing cry'd; That boy was blest,
Whose infant lips have drain'd a mother's breast;
But happier far are those (if such be known)
180 Whom both a father and a mother own:
But I, alas! hard fortune's utmost scorn,
Who ne'er knew parent, was an orphan born!
Some boys are rich by birth beyond all wants,
Belov'd by uncles, and kind good old aunts;

166 *japanning:* a mode of varnishing with a black gloss, introduced from Japan in the seventeenth century.

168 *Fleet-ditch:* The little River Fleet, now covered over, was still open and navigable up to Holborn Bridge. From there to its junction with the Thames it was known as the Fleet-ditch.

173 *common-shores:* the land on both sides of the Fleet-ditch, where refuse gathered or was dumped until the tide came up and washed it away.

174 *Holborn's fatal steep:* Cf. "A City Shower", p. 51, ll. 58-60. It was "fatal" because prisoners going from Newgate Prison to be hanged at Tyburn had to pass that way.

185 When time comes round, a Christmas-box they bear,
    And one day makes them rich for all the year.
    Had I the precepts of a Father's learn'd,
    Perhaps I then the coach-man's fare had earn'd,
    For lesser boys can drive; I thirsty stand
190 And see the double flaggon charge their hand,
    See them puff off the froth, and gulp amain,
    While with dry tongue I lick my lips in vain.
        While thus he fervent prays, the heaving tide
    In widen'd circles beats on either side;
195 The Goddess rose amid the inmost round,
    With wither'd turnip tops her temples crown'd;
    Low reach'd her dripping tresses, lank, and black
    As the smooth jet, or glossy raven's back;
    Around her waste a circling eel was twin'd,
200 Which bound her robe that hung in rags behind.
    Now beck'ning to the boy; she thus begun,
    Thy prayers are granted; weep no more, my son:
    Go thrive. At some frequented corner stand,
    This brush I give thee, grasp it in thy hand,
205 Temper the foot within this vase of oil,
    And let the little tripod aid thy toil;
    On this methinks I see the walking crew
    At thy request support the miry shoe,
    The foot grows black that was with dirt
        imbrown'd,
210 And in thy pocket gingling halfpence sound.
    The Goddess plunges swift beneath the flood,
    And dashes all around her show'rs of mud:
    The youth strait chose his post; the labour ply'd
    Where branching streets from Charing-cross divide;
215 His treble voice resounds along the *Meuse*,
    And White-hall echoes—*Clean your Honour's shoes.*

205 *Temper:* probably in the sense of bringing the leather to a suitable softness.

215 *the Meuse:* The Royal Mews stood on the site now occupied by the National Gallery. Originally used for keeping the King's falcons, they had become royal stables by Gay's time.

Like the sweet ballad, this amusing lay
Too long detains the walker on his way;
While he attends, new dangers round him throng;
220   The busy city asks instructive song.
   Where elevated o'er the gaping croud,
Clasp'd in the board the perjur'd head is bow'd,
Betimes retreat; here, thick as hailstones pour
Turnips, and half-hatch'd eggs, (a mingled show'r)
225   Among the rabble rain: Some random throw
May with the trickling yolk thy cheek o'erflow.

Of narrow
Streets.
   Though expedition bids, yet never stray
Where no rang'd posts defend the rugged way.
Here laden carts with thundring waggons meet,
230   Wheels clash with wheels, and bar the narrow street;
The lashing whip resounds, the horses strain,
And blood in anguish bursts the swelling vein.
O barb'rous men, your cruel breasts asswage,
Why vent ye on the gen'rous steed your rage?
235   Does not his service earn your daily bread?
Your wives, your children by his labours fed!
If, as the Samian taught, the soul revives,
And, shifting seats, in other bodies lives;
Severe shall be the brutal coachman's change,
240   Doom'd in a hackney horse the town to range:
Carmen, transform'd, the groaning load shall draw,
Whom other tyrants with the lash shall awe.

The most
inconvenient
Streets to
Walkers.
   Who would of Watling-street the dangers share,
When the broad pavement of Cheap-side is near?
Or who that rugged street would traverse o'er,
That stretches O Fleet-ditch, from thy black shore
To the Tow'r's moated walls? Here steams ascend
That, in mix'd fumes, the wrinkled nose offend.

217 *amusing:* interesting.

222 *the board:* the pillory.

228 *defend:* ward off.

237 *the Samian:* Pythagoras, who believed in the transmigration of souls
into other bodies after death.

245 *that rugged street:* "Thames-street" [Gay].

Where chandlers cauldrons boil; where fishy prey
250 Hide the wet stall, long absent from the sea;
And where the cleaver chops the heifer's spoil,
And where huge hogsheads sweat with trainy oil,
Thy breathing nostril hold; but how shall I
Pass, where in piles Cornavian cheeses lye;
255 Cheese, that the table's closing rites denies,
And bids me with th' unwilling chaplain rise.

The Pell-mell celebrated.

O bear me to the paths of fair Pell-mell,
Safe are thy pavements, grateful is thy smell!
At distance rolls along the gilded coach,
260 Nor sturdy carmen on thy walks encroach;
No lets would bar thy ways were chairs deny'd
The soft supports of laziness and pride;
Shops breathe perfumes, thro' sashes ribbons glow,
The mutual arms of ladies, and the beau.
265 Yet still ev'n here, when rains the passage hide,
Oft' the loose stone spirts up a muddy tide
Beneath thy careless foot; and from on high,
Where masons mount the ladder, fragments fly;
Mortar, and crumbled lime in show'rs descend,
270 And o'er thy head destructive tiles impend.

The Pleasure of walking through an Alley.

But sometimes let me leave the noisie roads,
And silent wander in the close abodes
Where wheels ne'er shake the ground; there pensive stray,
In studious thought, the long uncrouded way.
275 Here I remark each walker's diff'rent face,
And in their look their various bus'ness trace.

252 *trainy oil:* i.e. train-oil, obtained by boiling whale blubber.
254 *Cornavian:* "Cheshire anciently so called" [Gay].
256 *unwilling chaplain:* The private chaplain attached to a great household was allowed to sit down to dinner with the family, but was expected to withdraw after the first course.
257 *fair Pell-mell:* This fashionable residential street had been developed in the late seventeenth century.
261 *lets:* obstructions.   *chairs:* sedan chairs.
263 *sashes:* windows.   270 *impend:* hang threateningly.

The broker here his spacious beaver wears,
Upon his brow sit jealousies and cares;
Bent on some mortgage (to avoid reproach)
280   He seeks bye streets, and saves th' expensive coach.
Soft, at low doors, old letchers tap their cane,
For fair recluse, who travels Drury-lane;
Here roams uncomb'd the lavish rake, to shun
His Fleet-street draper's everlasting dun.

Inconveniences that attend those who are unacquainted with the Town.

Careful observers, studious of the town,
Shun the misfortunes that disgrace the clown;
Untempted, they contemn the jugler's feats,
Pass by the *Meuse*, nor try the thimble's cheats.
When drays bound high, they never cross behind,
Where bubbling yest is blown by gusts of wind:
And when up Ludgate-hill huge carts move slow,
Far from the straining steeds securely go,
Whose dashing hoofs behind them fling the mire,
And mark with muddy blots the gazing 'squire.
295   The Parthian thus his jav'lin backward throws,
And as he flies infests pursuing foes.

The thoughtless wits shall frequent forfeits pay,
Who 'gainst the centry's box discharge their tea.
Do thou some court, or secret corner seek,
300   Nor flush with shame the passing virgin's cheek.

Precepts vulgarly known.

Yet let me not descend to trivial song,
Nor vulgar circumstance my verse prolong;

277 *beaver:* fur hat.

282 *Drury-lane:* at this time a favourite haunt of prostitutes. Colley Cibber refers in one of his prologues to "the passage-walking Nymphs of Drury-lane".

288 *thimble's cheats:* "A Cheat commonly practis'd in the streets with three thimbles and a little ball" [Gay]. In thimblerig, as it is called, a pea is ostensibly placed under one of three thimbles and the bystander is invited to guess which one. The cheat is similar to the three-card trick.   *Meuse:* cf. l. 215.

295 *Parthian:* The Parthian military technique of discharging an arrow at the enemy while retiring at full speed has become proverbial.

296 *infests:* attacks.

Why should I teach the maid when torrents pour,
Her head to shelter from the sudden show'r?
305 Nature will best her ready hand inform,
With her spread petticoat to fence the storm.
Does not each walker know the warning sign,
When wisps of straw depend upon the twine
Cross the close street; that then the paver's art
310 Renews the ways, deny'd to coach and cart?
Who knows not that the coachman lashing by,
Oft' with his flourish cuts the heedless eye;
And when he takes his stand, to wait a fare,
His horses foreheads shun the winter's air?
315 Nor will I roam when summer's sultry rays
Parch the dry ground, and spread with dust the
     ways;
With whirling gusts the rapid atoms rise,
Smoak o'er the pavement, and involve the skies.
Frosty   Winter my theme confines; whose nitry wind
Weather.
320 Shall crust the slabby mire, and kennels bind;
She bids the snow descend in flaky sheets,
And in her hoary mantle cloath the streets.
Let not the virgin tread these slipp'ry roads,
The gath'ring fleece the hollow patten loads;
325 But if thy footsteps slide with clotted frost,
Strike off the breaking balls against the post.

308 *wisps of straw . . . twine:* From a statement in John Ashton's *Social Life in the Reign of Queen Anne*, 1882, ii, 157, it appears that this mode of indicating that a road was up was still the regular practice in the late nineteenth century.

314 *His horses foreheads, etc.:* i.e. the coachman covered their heads with a blanket.

318 *involve:* envelop.

319 *nitry:* nitrous, impregnated with saltpetre. Frost was thought to arise from nitre in the air crystallising the moisture. Cf. *Winter*, p. 180, l. 312.

320 *slabby:* cf. l. 92.

324 *patten:* an overshoe with a wooden sole, giving protection in wet weather by raising the wearer an inch or two from the ground.

On silent wheel the passing coaches roll;
Oft' look behind, and ward the threatning pole.
In harden'd orbs the school-boy moulds the snow,
330   To mark the coachman with a dext'rous throw.
Why do ye, boys, the kennel's surface spread,
To tempt with faithless pass the matron's tread?
How can ye laugh to see the damsel spurn,
Sink in your frauds, and her green stocking mourn?
335   At White's the harness'd chairman idly stands,
And swings around his waste his tingling hands:
The sempstress speeds to 'Change with red-tipt nose;
The Belgian stove beneath her footstool glows;
In half-whipt muslin needles useless lie,
340   And shuttle-cocks across the counter fly.
These sports warm harmless; why then will ye prove,
Deluded maids, the dang'rous flame of love?

The Dangers of Foot-ball.

    Where Covent-Garden's famous temple stands,
That boasts the work of Jones' immortal hands;
345   Columns with plain magnificence appear,
And graceful porches lead along the square:
Here oft' my course I bend, when lo! from far
I spy the furies of the foot-ball war:
The 'prentice quits his shop, to join the crew,
350   Encreasing crouds the flying game pursue.
Thus, as you roll the ball o'er snowy ground,
The gath'ring globe augments with ev'ry round.

328 *pole:* "a long tapering wooden shaft fitted to the fore-carriage of a vehicle" (O.E.D.). A coach was normally drawn by two or four horses.

333 *spurn:* trip, stumble.

335 *White's:* a famous chocolate house and gaming house in St. James's Street, later to become a club.

337 *'Change:* i.e. the New Exchange, a sort of bazaar of shops on the south side of the Strand.

338 *Belgian stove:* a stove for warming the feet.

339 *half-whipt:* In needlework to "whip" meant "to trim or ornament with embroidery" (O.E.D.). The muslin is "half-whipt" because the girls being cold, have taken to playing battledore and shuttlecock.

343 *temple:* the church of St. Paul's, Covent Garden, built by Inigo Jones, *c.* 1633.

But whither shall I run? the throng draws nigh,
The ball now skims the street, now soars on high;
355   The dext'rous glazier strong returns the bound,
      And gingling sashes on the pent-house sound.

An Episode of
the great Frost.   O roving Muse, recal that wond'rous year,
      When winter reign'd in bleak Britannia's air;
      When hoary Thames, with frosted oziers crown'd,
360   Was three long moons in icy fetters bound.
      The waterman, forlorn along the shore,
      Pensive reclines upon his useless oar,
      Sees harness'd steeds desert the stony town,
      And wander roads unstable, not their own:
365   Wheels o'er the harden'd waters smoothly glide,
      And rase with whiten'd tracks the slipp'ry tide.
      Here the fat cook piles high the blazing fire,
      And scarce the spit can turn the steer entire.
      Booths sudden hide the Thames, long streets appear,
370   And num'rous games proclaim the crouded fair.
      So when a gen'ral bids the martial train
      Spread their encampment o'er the spacious plain;
      Thick-rising tents a canvas city build,
      And the loud dice resound thro' all the field.
375   'Twas here the matron found a doleful fate:
      Let elegiac lay the woe relate,
      Soft as the breath of distant flutes, at hours
      When silent evening closes up the flow'rs;
      Lulling as falling water's hollow noise;
380   Indulging grief, like Philomela's voice.
          Doll ev'ry day had walk'd these treach'rous roads;
      Her neck grew warpt beneath autumnal loads

356 *sashes:* cf. l. 263.   *pent-house:* a lean-to building, shed, etc.

357 *that wond'rous year:* There was a hard frost in 1716, the year in which
Trivia was published; but Gay is almost certainly referring to the prolonged winter of 1709-10 when the Thames was frozen over for seven
weeks, or to the still more severe winter of 1683-4.

363 ff. Gay seems to be imitating Ovid, *Tristia*, iii, x, 31-4, and Virgil,
Georgics, iii, 361-2.

380 *Philomela's voice:* i.e. the nightingale.

Of various fruit; she now a basket bore,
That head, alas! shall basket bear no more.
385 Each booth she frequent past, in quest of gain,
And boys with pleasure heard her shrilling strain.
Ah Doll! all mortals must resign their breath,
And industry it self submit to death!
The cracking crystal yields, she sinks, she dyes,
390 Her head, chopt off, from her lost shoulders flies;
Pippins she cry'd, but death her voice confounds,
And pip-pip-pip along the ice resounds.
So when the Thracian furies Orpheus tore,
And left his bleeding trunk deform'd with gore,
395 His sever'd head floats down the silver tide,
His yet warm tongue for his lost consort cry'd;
Eurydice with quiv'ring voice he mourn'd,
And Heber's banks *Eurydice* return'd.

A Thaw.   But now the western gale the flood unbinds,
400 And black'ning clouds move on with warmer winds.
The wooden town its frail foundation leaves,
And Thames' full urn rolls down his plenteous
          waves;
From ev'ry penthouse streams the fleeting snow,
And with dissolving frost the pavements flow.

How to know   Experienc'd men, inur'd to city ways,
the Days of   Need not the Calendar to count their days.
the Week.   When through the town with slow and solemn air,
Led by the nostril, walks the muzled bear;
Behind him moves majestically dull,
410 The pride of Hockley-hole, the surly bull;

393 *Orpheus:* a famous musician who went down into Hades to bring back his wife Eurydice. Later, he was torn to pieces by Thracian women, and his head thrown into the River Hebrus. See Ovid, *Met.*, xi.

399 *gale:* wind.

402 *urn:* River-gods were represented in classical art as leaning upon, or pouring water from, an urn.

410 *Hockley-hole:* Hockley-in-the-Hole near Clerkenwell Green, where bulls and bears were baited, and prize fights of various kinds took place.

Learn hence the periods of the week to name,
Mondays and Thursdays are the days of game.
   When fishy stalls with double store are laid;
The golden-belly'd carp, the broad-finn'd maid,
415 Red-speckled trouts, the salmon's silver joul,
The joynted lobster, and unscaly soale,
And luscious 'scallops, to allure the tastes
Of rigid zealots to delicious fasts;
Wednesdays and Fridays you'll observe from hence,
420 Days, when our sires were doom'd to abstinence.
   When dirty waters from balconies drop,
And dext'rous damsels twirle the sprinkling mop,
And cleanse the spatter'd sash, and scrub the stairs;
Know Saturday's conclusive morn appears.

Remarks on the Crys of the Town.
   Successive crys the seasons' change declare,
And mark the monthly progress of the year.
Hark, how the streets with treble voices ring,
To sell the bounteous product of the spring!
Sweet-smelling flow'rs, and elder's early bud,
430 With nettle's tender shoots, to cleanse the blood:
And when June's thunder cools the sultry skies,
Ev'n Sundays are prophan'd by mackrell cries.
   Wallnuts the fruit'rer's hand, in autumn, stain,
Blue plumbs and juicy pears augment his gain;
435 Next oranges the longing boys entice,
To trust their copper fortunes to the dice.

Of Christmas.
   When rosemary, and bays, the Poet's crown,
Are bawl'd, in frequent cries, through all the town,

414 *maid:* the fish generally known as the skate.

415 *joul:* head and shoulders.

418 *religious zealots:* here, apparently, those who abstain from eating meat during Lent.

421 *balconies:* accented on the second syllable.

422 *sprinkling mop:* cf. "A Description of the Morning", p. 48, ll. 7-8.

424 *conclusive:* i.e. Saturday brings the week to a close.

429 *elder's . . . bud:* used for making salads.

432 *Sundays:* The sale of mackerel, because it does not keep well, was permitted on Sundays.

Then judge the festival of Christmas near,
440   Christmas, the joyous period of the year.
Now with bright holly all your temples strow,
With lawrel green, and sacred mistletoe.
Now, heav'n-born Charity, thy blessings shed;
Bid meagre Want uprear her sickly head:
445   Bid shiv'ring limbs be warm; let plenty's bowle
In humble roofs make glad the needy soul.
See, see, the heav'n-born maid her blessings shed;
Lo! meagre Want uprears her sickly head;
Cloath'd are the naked, and the needy glad,
450   While selfish Avarice alone is sad.

Precepts of Charity.

Proud coaches pass, regardless of the moan
Of infant orphans, and the widow's groan;
While Charity still moves the walker's mind,
His lib'ral purse relieves the lame and blind.
455   Judiciously thy half-pence are bestow'd,
Where the laborious beggar sweeps the road.
Whate'er you give, give ever at demand,
Nor let old-age long stretch his palsy'd hand.
Those who give late, are importun'd each day,
460   And still are teaz'd because they still delay.
If e'er the miser durst his farthings spare,
He thinly spreads them through the publick square,
Where, all beside the rail, rang'd beggars lie,
And from each other catch the doleful cry;
465   With heav'n, for two-pence, cheaply wipes his score,
Lifts up his eyes, and hasts to beggar more.
Where the brass knocker, wrapt in flannel band,
Forbids the thunder of the footman's hand;
Th' upholder, rueful harbinger of death,
470   Waits with impatience for the dying breath;

465 *wipes his score:* pays off his debt. (A "score" was chalked on a slate or door, etc., and wiped off when settled.)

467 *wrapt in flannel band:* cf. Pope, "*Epistle to Dr. Arbuthnot,*" l. 2: "Tie up the knocker, say I'm sick, I'm dead."

469 *upholder:* undertaker.

As vultures, o'er a camp, with hov'ring flight,
Snuff up the future carnage of the fight.
Here canst thou pass, unmindful of a pray'r,
That heav'n in mercy may thy brother spare?
475   Come, F***, sincere, experienc'd friend,
Thy briefs, thy deeds, and ev'n thy fees suspend;
Come let us leave the Temple's silent walls,
Me bus'ness to my distant lodging calls:
Through the long Strand together let us stray:
480   With thee conversing, I forget the way.
Behold that narrow street which steep descends,
Whose building to the slimy shore extends;
Here Arundel's fam'd structure rear'd its frame,
The street alone retains an empty name:
485   Where Titian's glowing paint the canvas warm'd,
And Raphael's fair design, with judgment, charm'd,
Now hangs the bell-man's song, and pasted here
The colour'd prints of Overton appear.
Where statues breath'd, the work of Phidias' hands,
490   A wooden pump, or lonely watch-house stands.
There Essex' stately pile adorn'd the shore,

475 *F****: William Fortescue (1687-1749), a lawyer and friend of Gay and Pope.

480 *With thee conversing:* cf. Milton, *Paradise Lost*, iv, 639: "With thee conversing, I forget all time."

483 *Arundel's fam'd structure:* Arundel House, the London residence of the Earls of Arundel, pulled down in 1678. The other great houses mentioned in ll. 491-2 had also been demolished by the time that Gay was writing. (Villers = Villiers, the family name of the Dukes of Buckingham.)

487 *the bellman's song:* The bellman was a night watchman, who called the hours during the night and also acted as a town crier. At Easter he would leave a copy of verses at the houses of the well-to-do in the hope of obtaining a gratuity.

488 *Overton:* John Overton (1640-1708?), a print-seller, well known for his mezzotints.

489 *statues breath'd:* a reminiscence of Virgil's *spirantia aera* (*Aeneid*, vi, 847).   *Phidias' hands:* Phidias, the famous Athenian sculptor, died 432 B.C.

There Cecil's, Bedford's, Villers', now no more.
Yet Burlington's fair palace still remains;
Beauty within, without proportion reigns.
495 Beneath his eye declining art revives,
The wall with animated picture lives;
There Hendel strikes the strings, the melting strain
Transports the soul, and thrills through ev'ry vein;
There oft' I enter (but with cleaner shoes)
500 For Burlington's belov'd by ev'ry Muse.

The Happiness of Walkers.

O ye associate walkers, O my friends,
Upon your state what happiness attends!
What, though no coach to frequent visit rolls,
Nor for your shilling chairmen sling their poles;
505 Yet still your nerves rheumatic pains defye,
Nor lazy jaundice dulls your saffron eye;
No wasting cough discharges sounds of death,
Nor wheezing asthma heaves in vain for breath;
Nor from your restless couch is heard the groan
510 Of burning gout, or sedentary stone.
Let others in the jolting coach confide,
Or in the leaky boat the Thames divide;
Or, box'd within the chair, contemn the street,
And trust their safety to another's feet,
515 Still let me walk; for oft' the sudden gale
Ruffles the tide, and shifts the dang'rous sail.
Then shall the passenger too late deplore
The whelming billow, and the faithless oar;
The drunken chairman in the kennel spurns,
520 The glasses shatters, and his charge o'erturns.

493 *Burlington's fair palace:* Burlington House, Piccadilly. Its owner, Richard Boyle, third Earl of Burlington, at this time a young man, became a great patron of the arts, and was himself an architect of some ability. He was a friend of both Gay and Pope, and Handel the composer, lived for three years in his house.

512 *the leaky boat:* The Thames watermen who rowed their fares up and down and across the River were almost the equivalent of twentieth-century taxi-drivers.

519 *spurns:* cf. l. 333.

Who can recount the coach's various harms,
The legs disjointed, and the broken arms?
   I've seen a beau, in some ill-fated hour,
When o'er the stones choak'd kennels swell the
      show'r

525 In gilded chariot loll; he with disdain
Views spatter'd passengers all drench'd in rain;
With mud fill'd high, the rumbling cart draws near,
Now rule thy prancing steeds, lac'd charioteer!
The dust-man lashes on with spiteful rage,

530 His pond'rous spokes thy painted wheel engage,
Crush'd is thy pride, down falls the shrieking beau,
The slabby pavement crystal fragments strow,
Black floods of mire th' embroider'd coat disgrace,
And mud enwraps the honours of his face.

535 So when dread Jove the son of Phœbus hurl'd,
Scarr'd with dark thunder, to the nether world;
The headstrong coursers tore the silver reins,
And the sun's beamy ruin gilds the plains.
   If the pale walker pant with weak'ning ills,

540 His sickly hand is stor'd with friendly bills:
From hence he learns the seventh-born doctor's fame,
From hence he learns the cheapest tailor's name.
   Shall the large mutton smoak upon your boards?
Such, Newgate's copious market best affords.

545 Would'st thou with mighty beef augment thy meal?
Seek Leaden-hall; St. James's sends thee veal.

525 *chariot:* a light four-wheeled carriage.

534 *honours:* The word *honores* in Latin poetry may have the meaning of "beauties", "ornaments". The "honours of the head" was fairly commonly used in neo-classical English poetry as a periphrasis for "hair". (Cf. *The Rape of the Lock*, p. 102, iv, 140.)

535 *son of Phœbus:* Phaeton, who persuaded his father Apollo to allow him to drive the chariot of the sun for one day—with disastrous results, for which he was punished in the way mentioned.

540 *bills:* advertising leaflets.

541 *seventh-born:* the doctor who could claim to be the seventh son of a seventh son was believed to be infallible.

Thames-street gives cheeses; Covent-garden fruits;
Moor-fields old books; and Monmouth-street old
    suits.
Hence may'st thou well supply the wants of life,
550 Support thy family, and cloath thy wife.
    Volumes on shelter'd stalls expanded lye,
And various science lures the learned eye;
The bending shelves with pond'rous scholiasts groan,
And deep divines to modern shops unknown:
555 Here, like the bee, that on industrious wing
Collects the various odours of the spring,
Walkers, at leisure, learning's flow'rs may spoil,
Nor watch the wasting of the midnight oil,
May morals snatch from Plutarch's tatter'd page,
560 A mildew'd Bacon, or Stagyra's sage.
Here saunt'ring prentices o'er Otway weep,
O'er Congreve smile, or over D** sleep;
Pleas'd sempstresses the *Lock's* fam'd *Rape* unfold,
And Squirts read Garth, 'till apozems grow cold.
565   O Lintot, let my labours obvious lie,
Rang'd on thy stall, for ev'ry curious eye;

552 *science:* learning.

553 *scholiasts:* commentators.

559 *Plutarch's . . . page:* Gay appears to be referring to Plutarch's *Moralia*, but may also have in mind his more famous *Lives*.

560 *Stagyra's sage:* Aristotle, who was born in Stagira, on the border of Macedonia.

561 *Otway:* Thomas Otway (1652-85), who wrote the pathetic tragedies of *The Orphan* and *Venice Preserved*.

562 *D**:* John Dennis (1657-1734), a writer of rather heavy tragedies, and a formidable critic.

563 *the Lock's fam'd Rape:* The Rape of the Lock had run rapidly through five editions by the time that Gay wrote this line.

564 *Squirts:* "The name of an Apothecary's boy, in the Poem of the Dispensary" [Gay]. *The Dispensary* (1699) was a highly popular poem by Sir Samuel Garth dealing with a quarrel between the apothecaries and the physicians, and ridiculing the apothecaries.   *apozems:* decoctions or infusions for medical use.

565 *Lintot:* Bernard Lintot, the publisher of Gay's poem.

So shall the poor these precepts *gratis* know,
And to my verse their future safeties owe.
   What walker shall his mean ambition fix
570 On the false lustre of a coach and six?
Let the vain virgin, lur'd by glaring show,
Sigh for the liv'ries of th' embroider'd beau.
   See yon bright chariot on its braces swing,
With Flanders mares, and on an arched spring;
575 That wretch, to gain an equipage and place,
Betray'd his sister to a lewd embrace.
This coach, that with the blazon'd 'scutcheon glows,
Vain of his unknown race, the coxcomb shows.
Here the brib'd lawyer, sunk in velvet, sleeps;
580 The starving orphan, as he passes, weeps;
There flames a fool, begirt with tinsell'd slaves,
Who wastes the wealth of a whole race of knaves.
That other, with a clustring train behind,
Owes his new honours to a sordid mind.
585 This next in court-fidelity excells,
The publick rifles, and his country sells.
May the proud chariot never be my fate,
If purchas'd at so mean, so dear a rate;
O rather give me sweet content on foot,
590 Wrapt in my virtue, and a good *Surtout*!

573 *braces:* strong leather straps by which the body of a carriage was suspended from its springs.

574 *Flanders mares:* Strong Flemish horses were in great demand for drawing the ponderous coaches of the period.

590 *Surtout:* overcoat.

THE BIRTH OF THE SQUIRE.
AN ECLOGUE

In imitation of the POLLIO of Virgil

VIRGIL's fourth eclogue is a vision of the coming of a new golden age, and this is directly related to the birth of a son to a distinguished Roman, C. Asinius Pollio, who was consul in 40 B.C. Gay's poem celebrates the birth of a booby son to a booby squire. To this extent his poem is a parody; but although there is some direct reference to Virgil's eclogue (e.g. the child learning of his father's past exploits), the imitation is for the most part general rather than explicit. The birth of the squire brings in an inverted golden age of hunting, of wenching, and, above all, of heavy drinking. For several generations the awkward and loutish country squire had been a favourite butt of English comedy, and Gay had therefore a long satirical tradition behind him. His own squire (who has a good deal of resemblance to the brutal Sullen in Farquhar's *The Beaux' Stratagem*) is drawn with rather less than Gay's usual good-natured detachment. For once he is not pulling any punches; the tone is one of distaste, even at times of frank disgust.

> Ye sylvan Muses, loftier strains recite,
> Not all in shades, and humble cotts delight.
> Hark! the bells ring; along the distant grounds
> The driving gales convey the swelling sounds;
> 5 Th' attentive swain, forgetful of his work,
> With gaping wonder, leans upon his fork.
> What sudden news alarms the waking morn?
> To the glad Squire a hopeful heir is born.
> Mourn, mourn, ye stags; and all ye beasts of chase,
> 10 This hour destruction brings on all your race:
> See the pleas'd tenants duteous off'rings bear,
> Turkeys and geese and grocer's sweetest ware;
> With the new health the pond'rous tankard flows,
> And old October reddens ev'ry nose.
> 15 Beagles and spaniels round his cradle stand,
> Kiss his moist lip and gently lick his hand;

4 *gales:* winds.
14 *October:* a beer or ale brewed in October.

He joys to hear the shrill horn's ecchoing sounds,
And learns to lisp the names of all the hounds.
With frothy ale to make his cup o'er-flow,
20 Barley shall in paternal acres grow;
The bee shall sip the fragrant dew from flow'rs,
To give metheglin for his morning hours;
For him the clustring hop shall climb the poles,
And his own orchard sparkle in his bowles.
25 His Sire's exploits he now with wonder hears,
The monstrous tales indulge his greedy ears;
How when youth strung his nerves and warm'd his veins,
He rode the mighty Nimrod of the plains:
He leads the staring infant through the hall,
30 Points out the horny spoils that grace the wall;
Tells, how this stag thro' three whole Countys fled,
What rivers swam, where bay'd, and where he bled.
Now he the wonders of the fox repeats,
Describes the desp'rate chase, and all his cheats;
35 How in one day beneath his furious speed,
He tir'd seven coursers of the fleetest breed;
How high the pale he leapt, how wide the ditch,
When the hound tore the haunches of the witch!
These stories which descend from son to son,
40 The forward boy shall one day make his own.
Ah, too fond mother, think the time draws nigh,
That calls the darling from thy tender eye;
How shall his spirit brook the rigid rules,
And the long tyranny of grammar schools?

22 *metheglin:* a drink made with honey and flavoured in various ways.

26 *indulge:* gratify.

28 *Nimrod:* the "mighty hunter" (*Genesis*, x, 9).

32 *bay'd:* A stag is "brought to bay" when the hounds catch up with him and he turns his head towards them.

37 *pale:* fence.

38 *witch:* "The most common accident to sportsmen; to hunt a witch in the shape of a hare" [Gay]. It was believed that witches sometimes took the form of a hare to mislead the hunters.

45   Let younger brothers o'er dull authors plod,
     Lash'd into Latin by the tingling rod;
     No, let him never feel that smart disgrace:
     Why should he wiser prove than all his race?
        When rip'ning youth with down o'ershades his chin,
50   And ev'ry female eye incites to sin;
     The milk-maid (thoughtless of her future shame)
     With smacking lip shall raise his guilty flame;
     The dairy, barn, the hay-loft and the grove
     Shall oft' be conscious of their stolen love.
55   But think, Priscilla, on that dreadful time,
     When pangs and watry qualms shall own thy crime;
     How wilt thou tremble when thy nipple's prest,
     To see the white drops bathe thy swelling breast!
     Nine moons shall publickly divulge thy shame,
60   And the young Squire forestall a father's name.
        When twice twelve times the reaper's sweeping hand
     With levell'd harvests has bestrown the land,
     On fam'd St. Hubert's feast, his winding horn
     Shall cheer the joyful hound and wake the morn:
65   This memorable day his eager speed
     Shall urge with bloody heel the rising steed.
     O check the foamy bit, nor tempt thy fate,
     Think on the murders of a five-bar gate!
     Yet prodigal of life, the leap he tries,
70   Low in the dust his groveling honour lies,
     Headlong he falls, and on the rugged stone
     Distorts his neck, and cracks the collar bone;
     O vent'rous youth, thy thirst of game allay,
     Mayst thou survive the perils of this day!
75   He shall survive; and in late years be sent
     To snore away Debates in Parliament.

45 *younger brothers:* The eldest son of a country gentleman commonly received little education since he was to inherit the estate. His younger brothers, who had to earn their own living, were more likely to be sent to one of the two universities or one of the inns-of-court.

63 *St. Hubert's feast:* St. Hubert was the patron saint of huntsmen.

The time shall come, when his more solid sense
With nod important shall the laws dispense;
A Justice with grave Justices shall sit,
80 He praise their wisdom, they admire his wit.
No greyhound shall attend the tenant's pace,
No rusty gun the farmer's chimney grace;
Salmons shall leave their covers void of fear,
Nor dread the thievish net or triple spear;
85 Poachers shall tremble at his awful name,
Whom vengeance now o'ertakes for murder'd game.
    Assist me, Bacchus, and ye drunken Pow'rs,
To sing his friendships and his midnight hours!
    Why dost thou glory in thy strength of beer,
90 Firm-cork'd, and mellow'd till the twentieth year;
Brew'd or when Phœbus warms the fleecy sign,
Or when his languid rays in Scorpio shine.
Thinks on the mischiefs which from hence have sprung!
It arms with curses dire the wrathful tongue;
95 Foul scandal to the lying lip affords,
And prompts the mem'ry with injurious words.
O where is wisdom, when by this o'erpower'd?
The State is censur'd, and the maid deflower'd!
And wilt thou still, O Squire, brew ale so strong?
100 Hear then the dictates of prophetic song.
    Methinks I see him in his hall appear,
Where the long table floats in clammy beer,
'Midst mugs and glasses shatter'd o'er the floor,
Dead-drunk his servile crew supinely snore;

78 *dispense:* administer.

81–6 *No greyhound . . . game:* Since the Restoration, strict game laws had been in force, designed to preserve shooting and fishing rights for the upper classes. Even freeholders of under one hundred pounds a year were not allowed to kill game on their own land. Enforcing the law against poachers was, in the eyes of the country justice, his chief function as a magistrate.

91–2 *fleecy sign . . . Scorpio:* The sun is in the sign of Aries (the Ram, the "fleecy sign") in March–April, and in Scorpio in October–November. Potent beers and ales—March beer and October ale (cf. l. 14)—were brewed at those two periods.

105   Triumphant, o'er the prostrate brutes he stands,
 The mighty bumper trembles in his hands;
 Boldly he drinks, and like his glorious Sires,
 In copious gulps of potent ale expires.

SWEET WILLIAM'S FAREWELL TO BLACK-EY'D SUSAN.

A BALLAD

SIMPLICITY did not come very easily to the eighteenth-century poet, but it presented no problems to Gay, who had an innocent gaiety of temperament that enabled him to write without affectation (although never without artifice) whenever the occasion demanded it. Compared to Carey's "Sally in our Alley" the following ballad is still mildly sophisticated: the cord sliding swiftly through William's "glowing hands" effectively distances the detached poet from the humble sailor. But at least Susan is not a "nymph", and William, although he has clearly been cleaned up a little and can talk to his sweetheart about "Africk's spicy gales", is still recognisably a sailor. The text is from *Poems on Several Occasions*, 1720.

 All in the Downs the fleet was moor'd,
  The streamers waving in the wind,
  When black-ey'd Susan came aboard.
   Oh! where shall I my true love find!
5 Tell me, ye jovial sailors, tell me true,
 If my sweet William sails among the crew.

 William, who high upon the yard,
  Rock'd with the billow to and fro,
  Soon as her well-known voice he heard,
10 He sigh'd and cast his eyes below.
 The cord slides swiftly through his glowing hands,
 And (quick as lightning) on the deck he stands.

 So the sweet lark, high-pois'd in air,
  Shuts close his pinions to his breast,
15 (If, chance, his mate's shrill call he hear)
  And drops at once into her nest.
 The noblest Captain in the British fleet,
 Might envy William's lip those kisses sweet.

O Susan, Susan, lovely dear,
20   My vows shall ever true remain;
Let me kiss off that falling tear,
    We only part to meet again.
Change, as ye list, ye winds; my heart shall be
The faithful compass that still points to thee.

25 Believe not what the landmen say,
        Who tempt with doubts thy constant mind:
    They'll tell thee, sailors, when away,
        In ev'ry port a mistress find.
    Yes, yes, believe them when they tell thee so,
30 For thou art present wheresoe'er I go.

    If to far India's coast we sail,
        Thy eyes are seen in di'monds bright,
    Thy breath is Africk's spicy gale,
        Thy skin is ivory, so white.
35 Thus ev'ry beauteous object that I view,
    Wakes in my soul some charm of lovely Sue.

    Though battel call me from thy arms,
        Let not my pretty Susan mourn;
    Though cannons roar, yet safe from harms,
40   William shall to his Dear return.
    Love turns aside the balls that round me fly,
    Lest precious tears should drop from Susan's eye.

    The boatswain gave the dreadful word,
        The sails their swelling bosom spread,
45 No longer must she stay aboard:
        They kiss'd, she sigh'd, he hung his head;
    Her less'ning boat unwilling rows to land:
        Adieu, she cries! and wav'd her lilly hand.

Anon

THE VICAR OF BRAY

THIS good-humoured satirical song about a time-serving parson embodies much of the history of England in five successive reigns, when the political scene kept altering abruptly owing to the personal policies of the last two Stuart kings, the Glorious Revolution of 1688, the reign of William and Mary when toleration for the Dissenters became possible, the reign of Queen Anne when the High Tories returned to power and reversed the process, and finally, on the death of Anne, the accession of George I and the triumph of the Whigs. Whenever the Tories were in power the doctrine of the divine right of kings and non-resistance to the royal authority found favour; when the Whigs were in office, such notions were regarded as an infringement of the Englishman's liberties, and the Dissenters, who found it impossible to conform to the worship of the Church of England, enjoyed at least a measure of toleration. This is neither a Whig nor a Tory song: on this occasion the two embattled political parties have called a truce, and have agreed to laugh together at the expense of the Church— or, at any rate, at the type of pliable and opportunist parson who veered like a weathercock with every wind of change. The author of "The Vicar of Bray" is unknown.

> In good King Charles's golden days,
>   When Loyalty no harm meant;
> A Furious High-Church Man I was,
>   And so I gain'd Preferment.
> 5 Unto my Flock I daily Preach'd,
>   Kings are by God appointed,
> And Damn'd are those who dare resist,
>   Or touch the Lord's Anointed.
>   And this is Law, I will maintain
> 10   Unto my Dying Day, Sir,
>   That whatsoever King shall Reign,
>   I will be Vicar of Bray, Sir!
>
> When Royal James possest the Crown,
>   And Popery grew in fashion;
> 15 The Penal Law I houted down,

15 *Penal Law:* the Test Acts of 1673 and 1678 directed against all those who were not members of the Church of England.   *houted:* hooted.

And read the Declaration:
The Church of Rome I found would fit
   Full well my Constitution,
And I had been a Jesuit,
20   But for the Revolution.
         And this is Law, &c.

When William our Deliverer came,
   To heal the Nation's Grievance,
I turned the Cat in Pan again,
25   And swore to him Allegiance:
Old Principles I did revoke,
   Set Conscience at a distance,
Passive Obedience is a Joke,
   A Jest is Non-resistance.
30   And this is Law, &c.

When glorious Anne became our Queen,
   The Church of England's Glory,
Another face of things was seen,
   And I became a Tory:
35   Occasional Conformists base
   I Damn'd, and Moderation,
And thought the Church in danger was,
   From such Prevarication.
         And this is Law, &c.

16 *the Declaration:* i.e. the Declaration of Indulgence, which James II ordered to be read in every cathedral and parish church on two successive Sundays in April 1688.

24 *turned the Cat in Pan:* changed sides.

31 *glorious Anne:* In her first speech from the throne the Queen had declared: "My own principles must always keep me entirely firm to the interests and religion of the Church of England, and will incline me to countenance those who have the truest zeal to support it."

35 *Occasional Conformists:* those Dissenters who, for the sake of holding some public office otherwise debarred to them, took communion occasionally in the Church of England. A bill to stop this practice was introduced early in the Queen's reign, and became law in 1711.

40 When George in Pudding time came o'er,
        And Moderate Men looked big, Sir,
    My Principles I chang'd once more,
        And so became a Whig, Sir:
    And thus Preferment I procur'd
45   From our Faith's Great Defender,
    And almost every day abjur'd
        The Pope, and the Pretender.
            And this is Law, &.

    The Illustrious House of Hannover,
50   And Protestant Succession,
    To these I lustily will swear,
        Whilst they can keep possession:
    For in my Faith, and Loyalty,
        I never once will faulter,
55 But George my Lawful King shall be,
        Except the Times shou'd alter.
            And this is Law, I will maintain
                Unto my Dying Day, Sir,
            That whatsoever King shall Reign,
60   I will be Vicar of Bray, Sir!

James Thomson

WINTER

THOMSON's *Winter* was first published in March 1726, when the poet, who had come south from Scotland in the previous spring, was twenty-five years old. The success of this poem led him to write *Summer* (1727), *Spring* (1728), and finally *Autumn* (1730), all four poems being then published together as *The Seasons*. According to Thomson himself, it was a poem on winter by his friend Robert Riccaltoun that first put the idea into his head of writing on that season; it also offered him a rather less hackneyed theme than spring or summer, and one that had appealed strongly to several of his Scots predecessors. For one who wished to dwell on such themes as

> exalt the Soul to solemn Thought,
> And heavenly musing,

winter gave him what he needed. The blank verse in which he had chosen to write was particularly well suited for those cumulative passages in which he was at his best, and enabled him to give free rein to his descriptions of the snowstorm and the great storm at sea (340 ff.). To the second edition of the poem Thomson added a rather polemical preface in which he touched on the frivolous nature of much modern verse, with its "forced unaffecting fancies, little glittering prettinesses, mixed turns of wit and expression". If poetry was once more to be restored to its ancient truth and purity, there could be no subject better fitted "to awake the poetical enthusiasm, the philosophical reflection, and the moral sentiment, than the works of Nature. Where can we meet with such variety, such beauty, such magnificence? All that enlarges and transports the soul! What more inspiring than a calm, wide survey of them?" It is a "calm, wide survey" that Thomson has given us in *Winter*, rising and falling in intensity with the natural development of his theme.

The text of the poem given here is that of the first edition, with the addition of one passage (ll. 233-43) introduced by the poet into the second edition of the same year. Thomson's first printer so peppered the page with commas as to make it almost impossible to read the poem (e.g. "In the red, evening, Sky"). These superfluous commas have been silently removed for the convenience of the reader. In later years Thomson continued to revise and add to *The Seasons*, and *Winter* finally grew to be a poem of 1,069 lines. Although his revisions were often happy, his additions tended to overload the poem and clog its movement. The impact of the original *Winter* on the mind of the reader is much sharper than that of later versions, and it is a more shapely poem.

> See! Winter comes, to rule the varied Year,
> Sullen, and sad; with all his rising Train,
> Vapours, and Clouds, and Storms: Be these my Theme,
> These, that exalt the Soul to solemn Thought,
> 5 And heavenly musing. Welcome kindred Glooms!
> Wish'd, wint'ry Horrors, hail!—With frequent Foot,
> Pleas'd have I, in my cheerful Morn of Life,
> When, nurs'd by careless Solitude, I liv'd,
> And sung of Nature with unceasing Joy,
> 10 Pleas'd have I wander'd thro' your rough Domains;
> Trod the pure, virgin Snows, my self as pure:
> Heard the Winds roar, and the big Torrent burst:
> Or seen the deep, fermenting Tempest brew'd
> In the red evening Sky.—Thus pass'd the Time,
> 15 Till, thro' the opening Chambers of the South,
> Look'd out the joyous Spring, look'd out, and smil'd.

Thee too, Inspirer of the toiling Swain!
Fair Autumn, yellow rob'd! I'll sing of thee,
Of thy last, temper'd Days, and sunny Calms;
20   When all the golden Hours are on the Wing,
Attending thy Retreat, and round thy Wain,
Slow-rolling, onward to the Southern Sky.

Behold! the well-pois'd Hornet, hovering, hangs
With quivering Pinions in the genial Blaze;
25   Flys off in airy Circles: then returns,
And hums, and dances to the beating Ray.
Nor shall the Man that musing walks alone,
And heedless strays within his radiant Lists,
Go unchastis'd away. . . . Sometimes a Fleece
30   Of Clouds, wide-scattering, with a lucid Veil,
Soft shadow o'er th' unruffled Face of Heaven;
And thro' their dewy Sluices shed the Sun,
With temper'd Influence down. Then is the Time
For those whom Wisdom and whom Nature charm,
35   To steal themselves from the degenerate Croud,
And soar above this little Scene of Things:
To tread low-thoughted Vice beneath their Feet:
To lay their Passions in a gentle Calm,
And woo lone Quiet in her silent Walks.

40   Now solitary and in pensive Guise,
Oft let me wander o'er the russet Mead,
Or thro' the pining Grove; where scarce is heard
One dying Strain, to chear the Woodman's Toil:
Sad Philomel, perchance, pours forth her Plaint,

28 *Lists:* an arena in which knights tilted against each other. The knight with his spear is a rather forced comparison for the hornet with its sting.

31 *Soft:* softly.

44 *Philomel:* Someone must have told Thomson that nightingales do not sing in the autumn, for in the second edition (1726) this line becomes: "Haply, some widdow'd Songster pours his Plaint." As a Scot recently arrived in England, Thomson had probably little or no first-hand knowledge of nightingales.

45 Far thro' the withering Copse. Mean while, the Leaves
   That late the Forest clad with lively Green,
   Nipt by the drizzly Night, and Sallow-hu'd,
   Fall, wavering, thro' the Air: or shower amain,
   Urg'd by the Breeze, that sobs amid the Boughs.
50 Then listening Hares forsake the rusling Woods,
   And, starting at the frequent Noise, escape
   To the rough Stubble and the rushy Fen.
   Then Woodcocks o'er the fluctuating Main,
   That glimmers to the Glimpses of the Moon,
55 Stretch their long Voyage to the woodland Glade:
   Where, wheeling with uncertain Flight, they mock
   The nimble Fowler's Aim.—Now Nature droops;
   Languish the living Herbs with pale Decay:
   And all the various Family of Flowers
60 Their sunny Robes resign. The falling Fruits
   Thro' the still Night forsake the Parent-Bough,
   That, in the first grey Glances of the Dawn,
   Looks wild, and wonders at the wintry Waste.

   The Year, yet pleasing, but declining fast,
65 Soft o'er the secret Soul in gentle Gales
   A Philosophic Melancholly breathes,
   And bears the swelling Thought aloft to Heaven.
   Then forming Fancy rouses to conceive
   What never mingled with the Vulgar's Dream:
70 Then wake the tender Pang, the pitying Tear,
   The Sigh for suffering Worth, the Wish prefer'd
   For Humankind, the Joy to see them bless'd,
   And all the Social Off-spring of the Heart!

53 *fluctuating:* in its literal sense of "rising and falling in waves" (Lat. *fluctus* = a wave).

58 *Herbs:* herbage, more especially grass.

65 *Gales:* breezes.

68 *forming:* creative.

69 *Vulgar's:* of the common sort.

71 *prefer'd:* put forward, offered.

Oh! bear me then to high, embowering Shades;
75 To twilight Groves, and visionary Vales;
To weeping Grottos, and to hoary Caves;
Where Angel-Forms are seen, and Voices heard,
Sigh'd in low Whispers that abstract the Soul
From outward Sense, far into Worlds remote.

80 Now, when the Western Sun withdraws the Day,
And humid Evening, gliding o'er the Sky,
In her chill Progress checks the straggling Beams,
And robs them of their gather'd, vapoury Prey,
Where Marshes stagnate, and where Rivers wind,
85 Cluster the rolling Fogs, and swim along
The dusky-mantled Lawn: then slow descend,
Once more to mingle with their Watry Friends.

The vivid Stars shine out in radiant Files;
And boundless Ether glows, till the fair Moon
90 Shows her broad Visage in the crimson'd East;
Now, stooping, seems to kiss the passing Cloud:
Now, o'er the pure Cerulean, rides sublime.
Wide the pale Deluge floats, with silver Waves,
O'er the sky'd Mountain, to the low-laid Vale;
95 From the white Rocks with dim Reflexion gleams,
And faintly glitters thro' the waving Shades.

All Night abundant Dews, unnoted, fall,
And, at Return of Morning, silver o'er
The Face of Mother-Earth; from every Branch
100 Depending, tremble the translucent Gems,
And quivering seem to fall away, yet cling,
And sparkle in the Sun, whose rising Eye,
With Fogs bedim'd, portends a beauteous Day.

86 *Lawn:* an open stretch of grassy land, a glade.
89 *Ether:* the upper regions of space beyond the clouds.
92 *Cerulean:* the blue (sky).
93 *pale Deluge:* i.e. the moonlight.
94 *sky'd:* in the skies.

     Now giddy Youth, whom headlong Passions fire,
105 Rouse the wild Game, and stain the guiltless Grove,
     With Violence and Death; yet call it Sport,
     To scatter Ruin thro' the Realms of Love,
     And Peace that thinks no Ill: But These the Muse,
     Whose Charity, unlimited, extends
110 As wide as Nature works, disdains to sing,
     Returning to her nobler Theme in view—

     For see! where Winter comes, himself confest,
     Striding the gloomy Blast. First Rains obscure
     Drive thro' the mingling Skies with Tempest foul;
115 Beat on the Mountain's Brow, and shake the Woods,
     That, sounding, wave below. The dreary Plain
     Lies overwhelm'd, and lost. The bellying Clouds
     Combine, and deepening into Night, shut up
     The Day's fair Face. The Wanderers of Heaven,
120 Each to his Home, retire; save those that love
     To take their Pastime in the troubled Air,
     And skimming flutter round the dimply Flood.
     The Cattle from th' untasted Fields return,
     And ask, with meaning Low, their wonted Stalls;
125 Or ruminate in the contiguous Shade:
     Thither the houshold feathery People croud,
     The crested Cock with all his female Train,
     Pensive and wet. Mean while, the Cottage-Swain
     Hangs o'er th' enlivening Blaze, and taleful there
130 Recounts his simple Frolic: Much he talks,
     And much he laughs, nor recks the Storm that blows
     Without, and rattles on his humble Roof.

     At last the muddy Deluge pours along,
     Resistless, roaring; dreadful down it comes

109 *Charity:* benevolence, love.

112 *himself confest:* i.e. with all the recognisable signs of winter.

122 *dimply:* breaking into dimples or ripples.

124 *Meaning low:* This was altered by Thomson in the second edition to "meaning Low", with the obvious intention of making it clear that "meaning" is an adjective and "low" a noun, and not *vice versa.*

135   From the chapt Mountain and the mossy Wild,
      Tumbling thro' Rocks abrupt, and sounding far:
      Then o'er the sanded Valley, floating, spreads,
      Calm, sluggish, silent; till again constrain'd,
      Betwixt two meeting Hills it burst a Way,
140   Where Rocks and Woods o'er hang the turbid Stream.
      There gathering triple Force, rapid and deep,
      It boils, and wheels, and foams, and thunders thro'.

      Nature! great Parent! whose directing Hand
      Rolls round the Seasons of the changeful Year,
145   How mighty! how majestick are thy Works!
      With what a pleasing Dread they swell the Soul,
      That sees astonish'd! and astonish'd sings!
      You too, ye Winds! that now begin to blow,
      With boisterous Sweep, I raise my Voice to you.
150   Where are your Stores, ye viewless Beings! say?
      Where your aerial Magazines reserv'd
      Against the Day of Tempest perilous?
      In what untravel'd Country of the Air,
      Hush'd in deep Silence, sleep you, when 'tis calm?

155   Late, in the louring Sky, red, fiery Streaks
      Begin to flush about; the reeling Clouds
      Stagger with dizzy Aim, as doubting yet
      Which Master to obey: while rising slow,
      Sad, in the Leaden-colour'd East, the Moon
160   Wears a bleak Circle round her sully'd Orb.
      Then issues forth the Storm with loud Control,
      And the thin Fabrick of the pillar'd Air
      O'erturns at once. Prone on th' uncertain Main
      Descends th' Etherial Force, and plows its Waves
165   With dreadful Rift: from the mid-Deep appears,
      Surge after Surge, the rising, wat'ry War.

135 *chapt:* full of fissures or cracks.

161 *Control:* domination, command.

162 *the thin Fabrick of the pillar'd Air:* Here, as in some other places, Thomson becomes almost Shakespearean.

Whitening, the angry Billows rowl immense,
And roar their Terrors through the shuddering Soul
Of feeble Man, amidst their Fury caught,
170 And, dash'd upon his Fate: Then, o'er the Cliff
Where dwells the Sea-Mew, unconfin'd they fly,
And hurrying swallow up the steril Shore.

The Mountain growls; and all its sturdy Sons
Stoop to the Bottom of the Rocks they shade:
175 Lone on its Midnight-Side and all aghast,
The dark, way-faring Stranger, breathless, toils,
And climbs against the Blast—
Low waves the rooted Forest, vex'd, and sheds
What of its leafy Honours yet remains.
180 Thus, struggling thro' the dissipated Grove,
The whirling Tempest raves along the Plain;
And on the Cottage thatcht, or lordly Dome,
Keen-fastening, shakes 'em to the solid Base.
Sleep, frighted, flies; the hollow Chimney howls,
185 The Windows rattle, and the Hinges creak.

Then, too, they say, thro' all the burthen'd Air,
Long Groans are heard, shrill Sounds, and distant Sighs,
That, murmur'd by the Demon of the Night,
Warn the devoted Wretch of Woe, and Death!
190 Wild Uproar lords it wide: the Clouds commixt
With Stars, swift-gliding, sweep along the Sky.
All Nature reels.—But hark! The Almighty speaks:
Instant the chidden Storm begins to pant,
And dies, at once, into a noiseless Calm.

171 *Sea-Mew:* the common seagull.

173 *Sons:* i.e. trees.

179 *Honours:* adornments (Lat. *honores*). Cf. Pope, *Odyssey*, xi, 235:
"The leafy honours scattering on the ground."

180 *dissipated:* scattered, disintegrated.

182 *Dome:* dwelling.

189 *devoted:* doomed.

195   As yet 'tis Midnight's Reign; the weary Clouds,
        Slow-meeting, mingle into solid Gloom:
        Now, while the drousy World lies lost in Sleep,
        Let me associate with the low-brow'd Night,
        And Contemplation, her sedate Compeer;
200   Let me shake off th' intrusive Cares of Day,
        And lay the medling Senses all aside.

        And now, ye lying Vanities of Life!
        You ever-tempting, ever-cheating Train!
        Where are you now? and what is your Amount?
205   Vexation, Disappointment, and Remorse.
        Sad, sickening Thought! and yet deluded Man,
        A Scene of wild, disjointed Visions past,
        And broken Slumbers, rises, still resolv'd,
        With new-flush'd Hopes to run your giddy Round.

210   Father of Light, and Life! thou Good Supreme!
        O! teach me what is Good! teach me thy self!
        Save me from Folly, Vanity and Vice,
        From every low Pursuit! and feed my Soul
        With Knowledge, conscious Peace, and Vertue pure,
215   Sacred, substantial, never-fading Bliss!

        Lo! from the livid East, or piercing North,
        Thick Clouds ascend, in whose capacious Womb
        A vapoury Deluge lies, to Snow congeal'd:
        Heavy they roll their fleecy World along;
220   And the Sky saddens with th' impending Storm.
        Thro' the hush'd Air the whitening Shower descends,
        At first thin-wavering; till at last the Flakes
        Fall broad and wide and fast, dimming the Day
        With a continual Flow. See! sudden, hoar'd,
225   The Woods beneath the stainless Burden bow,
        Blackning along the mazy Stream it melts;

198 *low-brow'd:* dark, gloomy.

209 *new-flush'd:* (1) sent up on the wing, as a spaniel flushes a covey of birds; or, less probably, (2) with the rosy flush of youth.

224 *hoar'd:* whitened.

Earth's universal Face, deep-hid and chill,
Is all one dazzling Waste. The Labourer-Ox
Stands cover'd o'er with Snow, and then demands
230 The Fruit of all his Toil. The Fowls of Heaven,
Tam'd by the cruel Season, croud around
The winnowing Store, and claim the little Boon
That Providence allows. The Red-Breast sole,
Wisely regardful of th' embroiling Sky,
235 In joyless Fields and thorny Thickets leaves
His shivering Fellows, and to trusted Man
His annual Visit pays: New to the Dome,
Against the Window beats; then brisk alights
On the warm Hearth, and, hopping o'er the Floor,
240 Eyes all the smiling Family askance,
And pecks, and starts, and wonders where he is:
Till, more familiar grown, the Table-Crumbs
Attract his slender Feet. The foodless Wilds
Pour forth their brown Inhabitants; the Hare,
245 Tho' timorous of Heart, and hard beset
By Death, in various Forms, dark Snares, and Dogs,
And more unpitying Men, the Garden seeks,
Urg'd on by fearless Want. The bleating Kind
Eye the bleak Heavens, and next, the glistening Earth,
250 With Looks of dumb Despair; then sad, dispers'd,
Dig for the wither'd Herb thro' Heaps of Snow.

Now, Shepherds, to your helpless Charge be kind;
Baffle the raging Year, and fill their Penns
With Food at will: lodge them below the Blast,
255 And watch them strict; for from the bellowing East
In this dire Season oft the Whirlwind's Wing
Sweeps up the Burthen of whole wintry Plains,
In one fierce Blast, and o'er th' unhappy Flocks,
Lodged in the Hollow of two neighbouring Hills,
260 The billowy Tempest whelms; till, upwards urg'd,
The Valley to a shining Mountain swells,
That curls its Wreaths amid the freezing Sky.

237 *Dome:* cf. l. 182.

Now, all amid the Rigours of the Year,
In the wild Depth of Winter, while without
265 The ceaseless Winds blow keen, be my Retreat
A rural, shelter'd, solitary Scene;
Where ruddy Fire and beaming Tapers join
To chase the chearless Gloom: there let me sit,
And hold high Converse with the mighty Dead,
270 Sages of ancient Time, as Gods rever'd,
As Gods beneficent, who blest Mankind
With Arts and Arms, and humaniz'd a World.
Rous'd at th' inspiring Thought—I throw aside
The long-liv'd Volume, and, deep-musing, hail
275 The sacred Shades that slowly-rising pass
Before my wondering Eyes—First, Socrates,
Truth's early Champion, Martyr for his God:
Solon, the next, who built his Commonweal
On Equity's firm Base: Lycurgus, then,
280 Severely good, and him of rugged Rome,
Numa, who soften'd her rapacious Sons.
Cimon, sweet-soul'd, and Aristides just.
Unconquer'd Cato, virtuous in Extreme;
With that attemper'd Heroe, mild and firm,

267 *Tapers:* candles.

278 *Solon:* c. 600 B.C. He reformed the laws of the Athenians.

279 *Lycurgus:* He performed a similar service for Sparta about 880 B.C.

281 *Numa:* Numa Pompilius, a philosopher who succeeded Romulus as King; he gave Rome many of its laws and institutions, and civilised its rude inhabitants.

282 *Cimon:* a brave and generous Athenian who utterly defeated the Persian fleet at Salamis (480 B.C.), and routed them on land on the same day.   *Aristides:* a celebrated Athenian of the fourth century B.C. whose integrity was such that he was always referred to as "the Just".

283 *Cato:* Marcus Cato Uticensis, d. 480 B.C., a great upholder of republican liberty, and therefore an opponent of Julius Caesar. He was "unconquered" because, rather than fall into Caesar's hands, he killed himself.   *in Extreme:* in extremity.

284 *Heroe:* i.e. Timoleon, a Corinthian, d. 337 B.C., who was such an enemy of tyrants that he slew his own brother.   *attemper'd:* equable, self-controlled.

285 Who wept the Brother, while the Tyrant bled.
Scipio, the humane Warrior, gently brave,
Fair Learning's Friend; who early sought the Shade,
To dwell with Innocence and Truth retir'd.
And, equal to the best, the Theban, He
290 Who, single, rais'd his Country into Fame.
Thousands behind, the Boast of Greece and Rome,
Whom Vertue owns, the Tribute of a Verse
Demand, but who can count the Stars of Heaven?
Who sing their Influence on this lower World?
295 But see who yonder comes! nor comes alone,
With sober State, and of majestic Mien,
The Sister Muses in his Train—'Tis He!
Maro! the best of Poets, and of Men!
Great Homer too appears, of daring Wing!
300 Parent of Song! and equal by his Side
The British Muse, join'd Hand in Hand, they walk,
Darkling, nor miss their Way to Fame's Ascent.

Society divine! Immortal Minds!
Still visit thus my Nights for you reserv'd,
305 And mount my soaring Soul to Deeds like yours.
Silence! thou lonely Power! the Door be thine:
See, on the hallow'd Hour, that none intrude,
Save Lycidas, the Friend, with Sense refin'd,
Learning digested well, exalted Faith,
310 Unstudy'd Wit, and Humour ever gay.

286 *Scipio:* i.e. Scipio Africanus, who defeated the Carthaginians in North Africa. He returned to Rome in triumph, but, disgusted with the ingratitude of his fellow citizens, retired into private life. His grandson, also called Africanus, had a strikingly similar career.

289 *the Theban:* Epaminondas, who defeated the Spartans at Leuctra, 371 B.C.

298 *Maro:* Virgil (Publius Virgilius Maro).

301 *the British Muse:* Milton.

302 *Darkling:* in the dark. Both Homer and Milton (in his old age) were blind.

305 *mount:* elevate.

Clear Frost succeeds, and thro' the blew Serene,
For Sight too fine, th' Ætherial Nitre flies,
To bake the Glebe, and bind the slip'ry Flood.
This of the wintry Season is the Prime;
315 Pure are the Days, and lustrous are the Nights,
Brighten'd with starry Worlds till then unseen.
Mean while the Orient, darkly red, breathes forth
An Icy Gale, that, in its mid Career,
Arrests the bickering Stream. The nightly Sky
320 And all her glowing Constellations pour
Their rigid Influence down: It freezes on
Till Morn late-rising o'er the drooping World
Lifts her pale Eye, unjoyous: then appears
The various Labour of the silent Night,
325 The pendant Isicle, the Frost-Work fair,
Where thousand Figures rise, the crusted Snow,
Tho' white, made whiter by the fining North.

On blithsome Frolics bent, the youthful Swains,
While every Work of Man is laid at Rest,
330 Rush o'er the watry Plains, and shuddering view
The fearful Deeps below: or with the Gun,
And faithful Spaniel, range the ravag'd Fields,
And, adding to the Ruins of the Year,
Distress the Feathery, or the Footed Game.

335 But hark! the nightly Winds with hollow Voice
Blow, blustering, from the South—the Frost subdu'd,

311 *Serene:* expanse of clear sky.

312 *Nitre:* cf. *Trivia*, p. 149, l. 319 *n*. In a later extended version of *Winter* Thomson has some speculations on the nature of frost, and concludes that it is caused by

Myriads of little salts, or hooked, or shaped
Like double wedges, and diffused immense
Through water, earth, and ether . . .

313 *bake the Glebe:* harden the soil.
327 *fining:* purifying.

Gradual resolves into a weeping Thaw.
Spotted, the Mountains shine: loose Sleet descends,
And floods the Country round: the Rivers swell,
340   Impatient for the Day—Those sullen Seas
That wash th' ungenial Pole will rest no more
Beneath the Shackles of the mighty North;
But, rousing all their Waves, resistless heave—
And hark!—the length'ning Roar continuous runs
345   Athwart the rifted Main; at once it bursts,
And piles a thousand Mountains to the Clouds!
Ill fares the Bark, the Wretches' last Resort,
That, lost amid the floating Fragments, moors
Beneath the Shelter of an Icy Isle;
350   While Night o'erwhelms the Sea, and Horror looks
More horrible. Can human Hearts endure
Th' assembled Mischiefs that besiege them round:
Unlist'ning Hunger, fainting Weariness,
The Roar of Winds and Waves, the Crush of Ice,
355   Now ceasing, now renew'd with louder Rage,
And bellowing round the Main: Nations remote,
Shook from their Midnight-Slumbers, deem they hear
Portentous Thunder in the troubled Sky.
More to embroil the Deep, Leviathan
360   And his unweildy Train in horrid Sport
Tempest the loosen'd Brine; while, thro' the Gloom,
Far from the dire, unhospitable Shore,

338 *spotted:* with patches of still unmelted snow.

340 *Impatient for the Day:* Thomson appears to have come to see that these words had little meaning, for he altered them in 1738 to "Of bonds impatient".

341 *ungenial:* unfavourable to growth.

353 *Unlist'ning Hunger:* Hunger (i.e. hungry wild beasts?) does not listen to the pleas of the starving. Alternatively, if Hunger, like Weariness, refers to the condition of the hungry man, "unlist'ning" may suggest his stupor. But Thomson must have been uneasy about this personification; in 1730 he substituted "Heart-gnawing Hunger".

361 *Tempest:* agitate violently.

The Lyon's Rage, the Wolf's sad Howl is heard,
And all the fell Society of Night.

365 Yet Providence, that ever-waking Eye,
Looks down with Pity on the fruitless Toil
Of Mortals lost to Hope, and lights them safe,
Thro' all this dreary Labyrinth of Fate.

'Tis done!—Dread Winter has subdu'd the Year,
370 And reigns, tremendous, o'er the desart Plains!
How dead the Vegetable Kingdom lies!
How dumb the Tuneful! Horror wide extends
His solitary Empire.—Now, fond Man!
Behold thy pictur'd Life: Pass some few Years,
375 Thy flow'ring   Spring, Thy   short-liv'd   Summer's
         Strength,
Thy sober Autumn, fading into Age,
And pale, concluding Winter shuts thy Scene,
And shrouds Thee in the Grave—where now are fled
Those Dreams of Greatness? those unsolid Hopes
380 Of Happiness? those Longings after Fame?
Those restless Cares? those busy, bustling Days?
Those Nights of secret Guilt? those veering Thoughts,
Flutt'ring 'twixt Good and Ill, that shar'd thy Life?
All now are vanish'd! Vertue, sole, survives,
385 Immortal, Mankind's never-failing Friend,
His Guide to Happiness on high—and see!
'Tis come, the Glorious Morn! the second Birth
Of Heaven, and Earth!—awakening Nature hears
Th' Almighty Trumpet's Voice, and starts to Life,
390 Renew'd, unfading. Now th' Eternal Scheme,
That Dark Perplexity, that Mystic Maze,
Which Sight cou'd never trace, nor Heart conceive,
To Reason's Eye refin'd clears up apace.
Angels and Men, astonish'd, pause—and dread
395 To travel thro' the Depths of Providence,

373 *fond:* foolish.
389 *Trumpet's Voice:* i.e. the Last Trump, when the dead shall rise from
the grave.

Untry'd, unbounded. Ye vain Learned! see,
And, prostrate in the Dust, adore that Power,
And Goodness oft arraign'd. See now the Cause
Why conscious Worth, oppress'd, in secret long
400 Mourn'd unregarded: Why the Good Man's Share
In Life was Gall and Bitterness of Soul:
Why the lone Widow and her Orphans pin'd
In starving Solitude; while Luxury
In Palaces lay prompting her low Thought
405 To form unreal Wants: why Heaven-born Faith,
And Charity, prime Grace! wore the red Marks
Of Persecution's Scourge: Why licens'd Pain,
That cruel Spoiler, that embosom'd Foe,
Imbitter'd all our Bliss. Ye Good Distrest!
410 Ye Noble Few! that here unbending stand
Beneath Life's Pressures . . . yet a little while,
And all your Woes are past. Time swiftly fleets,
And wish'd Eternity approaching brings
Life undecaying, Love without Allay,
415 Pure flowing Joy, and Happiness sincere.

Henry Carey

THE BALLAD OF SALLY IN OUR ALLEY

"SALLY IN OUR ALLEY" is what Browning would have called a dramatic
lyric. It is the love-song of an apprentice, and is therefore written in a vulgar
colloquial idiom ("let him bang his Belly-full". "The Days that's in the
Week", "As soon as Text [not "*the* text"] is named", etc.). In a note to the
poem Carey explained that it was based on his observation of a shoemaker's
apprentice on holiday with his sweetheart. He added, significantly, that
when the song was published its natural simplicity was very much ridiculed
by some of his friends, but none the less "it made its way into the polite
world, and amply recompensed him by the applause of the divine Addison,
who was pleased more than once to mention it with approbation." Since
Addison died in 1719 it was no doubt written some years before that.
The text is from Carey's *Poems on Several Occasions*, 1729.

Of all the Girls that are so smart
    There's none like pretty Sally,
She is the Darling of my Heart,
    And she lives in our Alley.
5 There is no Lady in the Land,
    Is half so sweet as Sally,
She is the Darling of my Heart,
    And she lives in our Alley.

Her Father he makes Cabbage-nets,
10   And through the Streets does cry 'em;
Her Mother she sells Laces long,
    To such as please to buy 'em:
But sure such Folks could ne'er beget
    So sweet a Girl as Sally!
15 She is the Darling of my Heart,
    And she lives in our Alley.

When she is by I leave my Work,
    (I love her so sincerely)
My Master comes like any Turk,
20   And bangs me most severely;
But, let him bang his Belly-full,
    I'll bear it all for Sally;
She is the Darling of my Heart,
    And she lives in our Alley.

25 Of all the Days that's in the Week,
    I dearly love but one Day,
And that's the Day that comes betwixt
    A Saturday and Monday;
For then I'm dress'd, all in my best,
30   To walk abroad with Sally;
She is the Darling of my Heart,
    And she lives in our Alley.

9 *Cabbage-nets:* nets used for boiling cabbages.

11 *Laces:* probably boot-laces, but perhaps also those used to draw together stays, bodices, etc.

My Master carries me to Church,
    And often am I blamed,
35 Because I leave him in the lurch,
    As soon as Text is named:
I leave the Church in Sermon time,
    And slink away to Sally;
She is the Darling of my Heart.
40   And she lives in our Alley.

When Christmas comes about again,
    O then I shall have Money;
I'll hoard it up, and box and all
    I'll give it to my Honey:
45 And, would it were ten thousand Pounds,
    I'd give it all to Sally;
She is the Darling of my Heart,
    And she lives in our Alley.

My Master and the Neighbours all
50   Make game of me and Sally;
And (but for her) I'd better be
    A Slave and row a Galley:
But when my seven long Years are out,
    O then I'll marry Sally!
55 O then we'll wed and then we'll bed,
    But not in our Alley.

EPIGRAMS

In an age in which so much of the poetry is marked by a witty turn of thought and phrase, it is not surprising to find that the epigram was cultivated with success. Characteristically, all those given here have their origin in a contemporary event or circumstance.

Joseph Trapp and Sir William Browne

The first epigram is usually attributed to Joseph Trapp (1679-1747), an Oxford man; the answer is by Sir William Browne (1692-1774), a Cambridge man. For many years after the accession of George I in 1714, Oxford University remained High Tory and even Jacobite, while Cambridge University was predominantly Whig and loyal to the Hanoverians. Early in his reign the new King presented Cambridge University with a valuable library of over 30,000 books and manuscripts formed by Bishop John Moore of Ely, and about the same time refused to accept an address from Oxford University. It was this circumstance that gave the occasion for the two epigrams.

I

The King, observing with judicious eyes,
The state of both his universities,
To Oxford sent a troop of horse; and why?
That learned body wanted loyalty:
To Cambridge books, as very well discerning
How much that loyal body wanted learning.

II

The King to Oxford sent a troop of horse,
For Tories own no argument but force;
With equal skill to Cambridge books he sent,
For Whigs admit no force but argument.

Samuel Wesley

ON THE SETTING UP MR. BUTLER'S MONUMENT IN WESTMINSTER ABBEY

SAMUEL WESLEY (1691-1739), a schoolmaster, was an elder brother of the better known John and Charles Wesley. The neglect of the author of *Hudibras* during his lifetime, although much exaggerated, had become almost proverbial. Wesley's epigram was occasioned by the monument raised to his memory in 1721 by the wealthy alderman, John Barber.

> While Butler, needy Wretch! was yet alive,
> No gen'rous Patron would a Dinner give:
> See him, when starv'd to Death and turn'd to Dust,
> Presented with a Monumental Bust!
> The Poet's Fate is here in Emblem shown;
> He ask'd for Bread, and he receiv'd a Stone.

ON COLLEY CIBBER BECOMING POET LAUREATE

ON December 3, 1730, Colley Cibber "had the Honour to kiss his Majesty's Hand (on his being appointed Poet-Laureat in the room of the Rev. Mr. Laurence Eusden, deceas'd) and was graciously received" (*The Evening Post*, December 3-5, 1730). This appointment gave rise to a small storm of ridicule and protest, including the following epigram, which is probably the work of Pope and which at all events he included among the notes to his *Dunciad*.

> In merry old England it once was a rule,
> The King had his Poet, and also his Fool:
> But now we're so frugal, I'd have you to know it,
> That Cibber can serve both for Fool and for Poet.

Lord Hervey

ON THE EARL OF BURLINGTON, AND HIS HOUSE AT CHISWICK

JOHN HERVEY, Baron Hervey of Ickworth (1696-1743), was Vice-Chamberlain in the royal household and the confidant of Queen Caroline. He was the author of the fascinating *Memoirs of the Reign of King George II*, first published in 1848. He also wrote some occasional verse, including the following epigram, which shows that Pope's admiration for Lord Burlington's ideas of architecture was not universally shared. Although the lines are said by the editor of *The New Foundling Hospital for Wit*, where they appeared, to refer to Burlington's Palladian villa at Chiswick, they might equally well be applied to Burlington House, Piccadilly, which he reconstructed on classical lines about 1716. Hervey is indebted to an epigram by Martial (xii, 50).

> Possess'd of one great Hall of State,
> Without one Room to sleep or eat;
> How well you build, let Flatt'ry tell,
> And all Mankind how ill you dwell.

Isaac Hawkins Browne

A PIPE OF TOBACCO: IN IMITATION OF SIX SEVERAL AUTHORS

THE growth of the reading public in the eighteenth century may be measured to some extent by the growth of parody as an amusing form of literary criticism. The development of parody as a literary kind depended on a sufficient number of readers being able to compare the work of the parodist with that of his victim. Among those poets whose work lent itself to satirical imitation was Ambrose Philips, whose poems written for and about children were frequently ridiculed. In 1736 Isaac Hawkins Browne (1706-60) made literary history by publishing a little volume of six separate parodies, which included one on Philips, and others on Colley Cibber, James Thomson, Edward Young, Pope and Swift, each poet celebrating the virtues of tobacco. Those on Philips and Pope are given here.

IMITATION II (Ambrose Philips)

> Little Tube of mighty Pow'r,
> Charmer of an idle Hour,
> Object of my warm Desire,
> Lip of Wax, and Eye of Fire:
> 5 And thy snowy taper Waste,
> With my Finger gently brac'd;
> And thy pretty swelling Crest,
> With my little Stopper prest;

1-4 *Little Tube . . . Fire:* Browne is parodying the first four lines of Philips' ode "To Signora Cuzzoni", which opens:

> Little Siren of the stage,
> Charmer of an idle age . . .

5-8 *And thy snowy . . . prest:* Cf. Philips, "To the Honourable Miss Carteret", ll. 41-4:

> Then the taper-moulded waste
> With a span of ribbon braced,
> And the swell of either breast,
> And the wide high-vaulted chest.

The line, "Happy thrice, and thrice again", comes from the same poem, l. 55. Browne also parodies Philips's habit of repetition.

And the sweetest Bliss of Blisses,
10 Breathing from thy balmy Kisses.
Happy thrice, and thrice agen,
Happiest he of happy Men;
Who when agen the Night returns,
When agen the Taper burns;
15 When agen the Cricket's gay,
(Little Cricket, full of Play)
Can afford his Tube to feed
With the fragrant Indian Weed:
Pleasure for a Nose divine,
20 Incense of the God of Wine.
Happy thrice, and thrice agen,
Happiest he of happy Men.

IMITATION V (Alexander Pope)

Blest Leaf! whose aromatic Gales dispense
To Templars Modesty, to Parsons Sense:
So raptur'd Priests, at fam'd Dodona's Shrine
Drank Inspiration from the Steam divine.
5 Poison that cures, a Vapour that affords
Content, more solid than the Smile of Lords:
Rest to the Weary, to the Hungry Food,
The last kind refuge of the Wise and Good.
Inspir'd by Thee, dull Cits adjust the Scale
10 Of Europe's Peace, when other Statesmen fail.
By Thee protected, and thy Sister, Beer,
Poets rejoice, nor think the Bailiff near.
Nor less, the Critic owns thy genial Aid,
While supperless he plies the piddling Trade.
15 What though to Love and soft Delights a Foe,
By Ladies hated, hated by the Beau,

3 *Dodona's Shrine:* a celebrated grove and temple in Epinus where there was a famous oracle of Jupiter.

9 *Cits:* citizens (settling the affairs of the nation in a coffee-house).

Yet social Freedom, long to Courts unknown,
Fair Health, fair Truth, and Virtue are thy own.
Come to thy Poet, come with healing Wings,
20 And let me taste Thee unexcis'd by Kings.

20 *unexcis'd:* In 1733 Sir Robert Walpole brought in, but (owing to intense opposition) soon dropped, an Excise Bill which would have brought the tobacco duty under the laws of the excise.

Philip Dormer Stanhope
Earl of Chesterfield

VERSES WRITTEN IN A LADY'S SHERLOCK "UPON DEATH"

LORD CHESTERFIELD inherited much of the wit and good sense of his famous grandfather, the Marquis of Halifax. As a writer he is best known for the letters that he wrote to his natural son, Philip Stanhope, over whose education he took the greatest possible care. Chesterfield's wit found brilliant expression in his conversation, but also from time to time in such verses as those given here, which have all the poise and the well-bred turn of the polite man of letters. This is not a concealed love-poem: Chesterfield is not really concerned about the lady, but very much concerned about striking an elegant attitude and making a witty point. The book that was absorbing the lady's attention was *A Practical Discourse concerning Death* by William Sherlock, D.D., which was a religious bestseller of the late seventeenth and early eighteenth centuries. The Verses first appeared in *The Gentleman's Magazine*, May 1733.

Mistaken fair, lay Sherlock by,
   His doctrine is deceiving;
For, whilst he teaches us to die,
   He cheats us of our living.

5 To die's a lesson we shall know
   Too soon, without a master;
Then let us only study now
   How we may live the faster.

To live's to love, to bless, be bless'd
10   With mutual inclination;
Share then my ardour in your breast,
And kindly meet my passion.

But if thus bless'd I may not live,
And pity you deny,
15   To me, at least, your Sherlock give,
'Tis I must learn to die.